CASANOVALTA

A Tuscan Farmhouse

A Memoir
by Anita Eubank

My Life in Italy with Architect
Craig Ellwood

Book Designer: Mary Meade
Art Director, Reader: Sheridan Sansegundo
Editorial Assist: Susan Fassberg
Cover & Title Page Illustrations: Brenda Eubank-Ahrens
Casanovalta Recipes Illustrations: Claire Ryle Garrison
Graphic Designer: Claudia Castillo
Author's Photograph: Vivien Ahrens

Book available for purchase at amazon.com and bookshop.org.
First edition:

*I dedicate this book to the angels who surround and
bless me always, my daddy among them—and to my
close circle of family and friends who are my
everyday angels. Thank you—I love you!*

Contents

The Beginning

T HIS IS A STORY ABOUT A house, a very old house (despite being named *Casa Novalta*, "new high house") perched high on a hill in Tuscany. Abandoned for years, *Casanovalta* found new life when a young woman fell in love with it and with her partner, an architect, restored it and opened its spaces to let in more light.

That is how it all began.

Rediscovery

PRESENT DAY

C AN YOU IMAGINE MY SURPRISE WHEN, out of the blue, I received this text through Facebook Messenger on June 15, 2021:

"Dear Anita Eubank, my name is Gabriele Cirami, and I'm an architect working with the University of Sant-Luc (Bruxelles) on an exhibition project, Houses Like Me: Italian Intellectuals and Domestic Spaces. We're quite interested in the house that you and your ex-husband, Craig Ellwood, restored in Tuscany (Pergine Valdarno). It could be an amazing study—exploring a place you called home—and we would love the opportunity to hear some stories about your time there. May I contact you for an interview and for some information about the house in Tuscany? Hoping to hear from you. Sending my best regards, Gabriele"

What followed was a year of intense correspondence with the young Florentine architect, Gabriele Cirami. We exchanged countless emails, conducted a recorded interview with his professor, Roberto Zancan, and his colleagues, and ultimately celebrated the culmination of our efforts at an exhibition in Brussels in May 2022, the installation designed by Gabriele. The exhibition was titled *Altre Case Come Me: Intelletuali e Spazio Domestico in Italia (Other Houses Like Me: Intellectuals and Domestic Space in Italy)*, which was also the title of the accompanying book in progress.

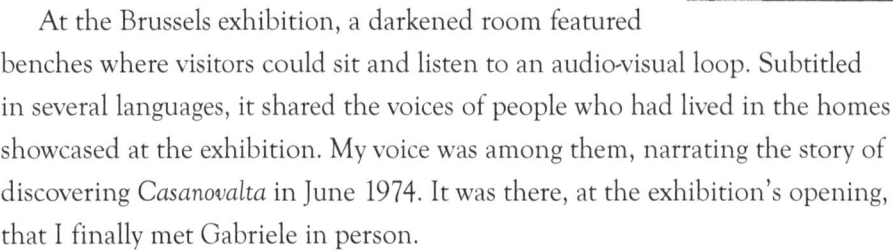

During our exchanges, I sent Gabriele historic photographs of *Casanovalta*, scans of the original design drawings I had made, including details of doors, windows, cabinetry, and furniture, as well as excerpts from my private journal recounting my life with Craig at *Casanovalta*.

At the Brussels exhibition, a darkened room featured benches where visitors could sit and listen to an audio-visual loop. Subtitled in several languages, it shared the voices of people who had lived in the homes showcased at the exhibition. My voice was among them, narrating the story of discovering *Casanovalta* in June 1974. It was there, at the exhibition's opening, that I finally met Gabriele in person.

With great animation, I shared my memories:

"There was a fine art gallery owner in Los Angeles named Felix Landau. He had moved to Paris and was a friend of my husband, Craig Ellwood. Felix had purchased a country house in Tuscany, and another property for investment. He suggested that Craig take a look at this second property—a ruin on a hilltop called "Casanovalta." In 1974, while on a romantic holiday in Italy, Craig and I decided to visit it. We drove his Dino Spyder Ferrari from Modena down to Napoli, Capri, and back up the coast

through Porto Ercole, the Maremma, and Monte Argentario.
Driving inland, we finally arrived at Pergine Valdarno.

A local farmer named Giovacchino Lunghi served as the
caretaker. Our Ferrari couldn't navigate the steep hill leading
to the property, so Giovacchino drove us up in his Fiat. As we
crested the hill, there it was—a ruin nestled into the side of the
slope—constructed of stone, terra cotta, and wooden beams.
Unlike a typical box-like Tuscan structure, this house appeared to
blend into the landscape. I felt as if I was struck by lightning! I leapt across
the meadow crying, 'Bellisima, bellisima!' I hugged the sun-warmed stone,
pressing my cheek against it, and felt the house's heartbeat. It was love at first
sight!"

This collaboration with Gabriele and Roberto awakened in me a desire to share
my story in a book of my own, drawing from my journal to recount an era of
Tuscany that no longer exists. It was a gentler, more rustic *Toscana,* filled with
artists, writers, sculptors, retired colonels, diplomats, local farmers, craftsmen,
and laborers—hardworking, sometimes cunning, but always generous in
hospitality and conversation.

I had been interviewed previously by the architect and architectural
historian Neil Jackson, whose award winning *California Modern: The Architecture*

 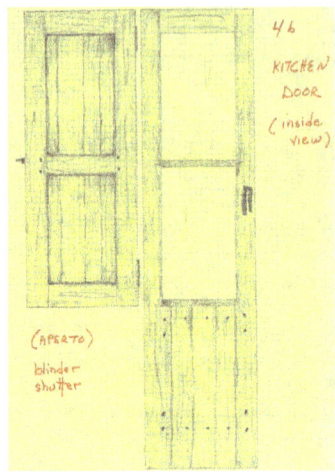 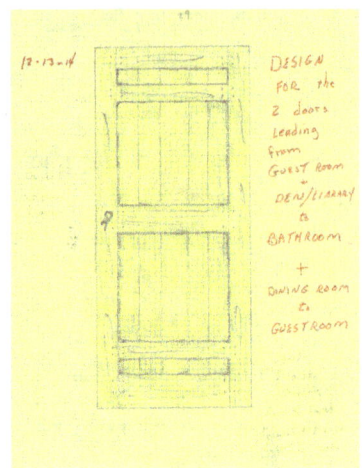

of *Craig Ellwood* (Princeton University Press 2003) featured a chapter on *Casanovalta*. Rizzoli Publishers also released *Making LA Modern: Craig Ellwood–Myth/Man/Designer* in 2018, edited by Michael Boyd, with art historian Jeffrey Head contributing a chapter on Craig's art. While these works captured aspects of Craig's life and career, none delved as intimately as Gabriele into what it was actually like to live at *Casanovalta*.

Roberto's book and Gabriele's exhibition focused on the lived experiences of Italian writers, artists, and filmmakers in the personal spaces they had lovingly restored or created. Among the homes featured were those of Michelangelo Antonioni, Giuseppi Berto, Luca Ronconi, Pier Paolo Pasolini, and Craig Ellwood. Their approach combined architectural analysis with firsthand narratives, as highlighted in this passage:

> "*These interpretations are accompanied by two series of interviews. The first series presents meetings with those who created or were close to the design of these houses–architects and designers who collaborated with the clients, such as Dante Bini and Dante Ferretti, or scholars who deeply studied these biographies. The second series focuses on dialogues with those who lived in these spaces or frequented them for long periods. These interviews with Antonia Berto, Anita Eubank, Marco Loporfido, and Anna Zoppo add insights, details, and anecdotes, offering a firsthand opportunity to verify and expand the interpretive essays, while refuting uncertainties.*"

> –*Altre Case Come Me: Intellettuali e Spazio Domestico in Italia*,
> Roberto Zancan, ed. (translated from Italian)

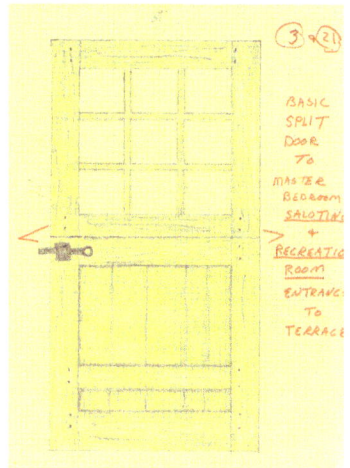

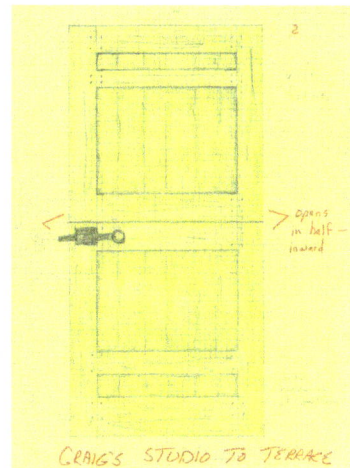

Inspired by this project, I want to tell the full story of restoring a Renaissance-era Tuscan farmhouse, dated 1531, and share the colorful characters and memorable experiences that shaped our lives there. From rubbing shoulders with distinguished neighbors to navigating the quirks of tireless yet sometimes exasperating workers, the journey was as challenging as it was rewarding.

One of the things I loved most about *Casanovalta* ("new high house") was its uniqueness. The rural farmers (*contadini*) built it of local stone, timber from the chestnut tree (*castagna*), and hearth-baked tiles. They tucked the house into the side of the hill in a non-traditional manner to protect themselves and their livestock from the winds which swept up the hill from the valley below.

Thus, in an architectural statement ahead of its time—instead of being a square box—*Casanovalta* was uniquely a "split-level" home. The three stories gave the appearance of two with the lower level, used primarily for sheep stalls, set down the hill. The charming third story, which had once served as the cheese room, was located behind the central chimney and accessed by a narrow stone stairway set in the wall beside the kitchen fireplace. The room had a whimsical pop-up roofline and a small window facing towards a row of cypress trees bordering the upper field.

In the early days of the restoration, before *Casanovalta* was habitable, we stayed at a small country inn called Hotel Ambra in the village of Ambra. The owners often roasted whole wild boars stuffed with slices of garlic and sprigs of rosemary, filling the hotel with mouth-watering aromas as I sketched to-scale designs for the house's doors, windows, cabinetry, furniture, and even the chimney pots. A hunting reserve surrounded *Casanovalta* and sadly, the hunters had burned

all its doors and windows to make their grilled lunches. Craig entrusted me with these designs, saying I had the ability to "think old." Meanwhile, he focused on creating arches to open the spaces between the kitchen, dining room, and living rooms. In the old barn, which became his art studio, he designed the largest arch possible in the north end to let in the light.

We embraced "living the dream" and devoted ourselves to the arduous task of reconstructing an ancient house which had no water, no toilets, no electricity, no telephone, and no heating system—aside from one cavernous kitchen fireplace. Felix Landau, who had introduced us to the property, disappeared to Paris leaving us to manage on our own. Salvation came in the form of Osvaldo Righi, a charming but mercurial Neapolitan aristocrat who lived in a castle named *Cennina* above the village of Ambra. Osvaldo, always in need of funds for his own 12th century restoration project, offered to act as our translator and coordinator. While his fiery personality sometimes caused more problems than he solved, his network proved invaluable. Determined to be less reliant on him, we hastily did our best to learn Italian. I joked that my hand was shaped in a permanent "crab claw" from holding my fat Caselli dictionary.

Craig and I married in Los Angeles on March 15, 1978. By June, we were back in Italy spurring on the construction workers to even greater productivity with the promise of a fabulous party, which we called the "*festa matrimoniale*," to celebrate our marriage and reward their hard work.

Once the house became habitable, we hosted a one-of-a-kind party. Two of the local butchers turned a whole lamb on a spit over the kitchen fireplace, and we also feasted on an entire roasted pig. Chianti and Pinot Grigio flowed like spring-water. The barn-turned-art-studio transformed into a vibrant venue when Craig filled it with yellow wildflowers, *ginestra* (Scotch broom) which the locals called *maggio* (flowers that bloom in May). Friends and family came from across Europe—and of course, every local neighbor and worker on the house. It was a magical night to remember—and the beginning of a new chapter in our Tuscan adventure.

Life at Casanovalta

THIS WAS HOW WE DISCOVERED CASANOVALTA on its hilltop perch, gazing across to the majestic Pratomagno mountains—a range framed by the Arno River on both sides, shaping the lush Valdarno valley to the west and the serene Casentino region to the east. The farmhouse itself, weathered and open to the elements, had lost its doors and windows, and many of its roof tiles were broken. Craig and I thought it was the most beautiful thing we had ever seen.

Before restoration began, *Casanovalta* had a mismatched pair of kitchen windows and a solitary chimney as the kitchen fireplace vent. The house seemed engulfed in thickets of nettles and brambles, as nature had reclaimed its territory.

In the early days of renovation, the contractor removed the entire roof, opening *Casanovalta* dramatically to sky and sunlight. Rotten timbers were replaced by robust chestnut tree trunk beams and flat terracotta ceiling tiles—and the stone wall was carefully dismantled to frame a breathtaking view.

With a gaping hole carved into the great north-facing stone wall, we had a magnificent view of rolling hills and the Arno valley below. I designed the window's proportions—six feet by three— to elegantly echo the kitchen window, uniting the spaces.

At this stage, the living room was taking shape beautifully—a generous lintel crowned the newly formed window, arches gracefully opened and connected spaces, and the fireplace mantel displayed its new grandeur. In front of the fireplace, a humble plank table on cement blocks hinted at future social gatherings. The walls were smooth with fresh plaster—

crafted by workers instructed by Craig to "plaster like their grandmother would do it." He wanted a rustic texture.

With its freshly tiled roof and perky new chimney pots, (which I styled according to local tradition), *Casanovalta* began to reclaim its dignity. The cluster of chimney pots indicated that three additional fireplaces now adorned and served the house. Rich wood lintels stood above the living room, dining room, and bedroom windows, but they were all awaiting their wooden frames.

We knocked a hole through the thick stone wall of the back bedroom and created an irregular stone staircase which ascended to the old cheese room—now charmingly reimagined as the main bathroom.

Craig savored grilling pork chops over glowing embers in the spacious kitchen fireplace, gently stoking the fire with a sturdy stick. A glass of robust Chianti never failed to inspire the cook.

Hanging on the art barn's wall was a large stretched canvas—a meticulous

tapestry of taped lines, rectangular shapes, and vibrant acrylic hues—part of Craig's hard-edge series tenderly titled "*Tesoruccio*" (Little Treasure), his affectionate nickname for me.

Craig delighted in gathering the abundant wildflowers which bloomed all around *Casanovalta,* filling our home with fragrant bouquets that captured the essence of the Tuscan countryside.

One of my greatest pleasures was to sit atop the sun-warmed terrace walls, gazing dreamily into the lush valley below, jotting reflections in my journal, or simply resting between daily household tasks.

Our wooden lattice window at the sheep-stall level, typical of Tuscan farmhouses, evoked a simpler past. Animals had sheltered in this lower stable, their body warmth rising to comfort the inhabitants above during cold winter nights.

The great stone lintels, above and below the bathroom window, embodied the beauty and simplicity of the ancient farmhouse.

By candlelight, the living room became a space of quiet intimacy— the gentle glow highlighting our cozy built-in sofa, romantic window, and the welcoming presence of our grand fireplace.

Our living room fireplace expressed the spirit of traditional Tuscan homes, boasting a broad wooden mantel, triangular plaster hood, and stone base harmoniously assembled. Craig handpicked stones for the mantel's braces, complemented by a black metal mesh fire screen forged by Italo, our talented local ironmonger. (Italo also made the metal dampers to all the fireplaces). Even though Craig said I had the ability to "think old," he is the one

who styled the tableau of the Etruscan foot, rustic cow bell hanging on the wall, and antique key display on the fireplace mantlepiece.

The completed living room became our beloved sanctuary, highlighted by its luminous window above the inviting built-in plaster sofa. Local carpenters, the skilled Maddii brothers, crafted the chestnut window frames and the low coffee table—while I carefully hand-stitched the sofa cushions from Florentine fabrics, brown wide wale corduroy, and terra cotta linen. I also acid washed, oiled, and waxed the tile floors.

The cheerful kitchen window, (gracefully symmetric with the living room), stretched generously above the sink, accordion-opening to let in Tuscan sunshine and gentle breezes. Our carpenters' golden chestnut window

frames, and Craig's meticulously designed five-hardwood countertops, turned everyday cooking into a sensory pleasure. The wooden doors, seen here at the lower level, led to the furnace and a laundry room.

Bathed in warm golden hues, *Casanovalta's* chestnut windows and ochre stone terraces, (built at last), glowed in harmony with the meadow bursting with scarlet poppies, wild grasses, and stinging nettles—nature's palette surrounding our lovingly restored home.

The Tuscan Journal

INTRODUCTION

THESE ARE MY PRIVATE JOURNAL ENTRIES from the two consecutive years I spent living in Italy with my husband, Craig Ellwood, from 1982 to 1983, as we entered the final stages of restoring our ancient Tuscan farmhouse, *Casanovalta*. Prior to that, we had traveled to Italy only in spring, summer, and early fall months which we dedicated to working tirelessly on the house. Over those seven years, Craig spent long hours painting in his art studio—the former barn. Just a year before, in October 1981, he had had his first major exhibit at the Lorenzelli Gallery in Milan.

By 1982, we decided to experience life in Tuscany year-round. My journal was born out of my struggle to adapt, to hold onto my sense of self, and to navigate the realities of our remote home. Through writing, I was able to keep my sometimes flagging spirit alive, and express the highs and the lows—the humor and the heartache—of facing the seemingly endless task of restoration, acid washing, oiling, and waxing the vast tile floors, and enduring a winter in a 500-year-old stone house, without any form of telecommunication, adequate heat, or any certainty that we'd emerge from the experience intact. It was not an easy season—but as the shining dawn always follows the dark night—spring, with its budding hope, really did come at last.

❧ *1982* ❧

Fall

October 3

Let me begin by saying that yesterday, Burbui, our furnace man, a dark haired and rather dapper gentleman, came for the second time to fix the *brusciatore* (furnace) so we could have hot water. We've been without hot water ever since Craig and I arrived from California on September 10th. Last weekend, we went to Terme Petriolo, a nearby hot springs, just to get clean and soak in a hot tub. We feel renewed and ready to tackle our problems and challenges once more.

October 26

I just hung the laundry on a clothes rack in front of the kitchen fireplace to dry. It's amazing how effective that can be and how many clothes I can fit on there. The only problem is that our clothes constantly smell of smoke. Craig and I have given up hope for sunshine. I guess it will rain endlessly all winter long.

    A stiff wind is blowing the smoke back down the chimneys. I'm trying to read but my eyes are blinded by smoke. Our use of firewood seems scandalous—all that lovely oak.

HALLOWEEN

October 31

Last night, I felt like a lost soul again. Standing in the high field above our house in the dark of Halloween night I yelled, "Go away!" and suddenly, I felt much better. Could other lost souls have been prowling around coming to haunt me?

Here in the cloudless morning light as I write this journal, my beloved long-haired white Angora cat, Muffin, has climbed back in the window from the steep tile roof to give me some "good morning loving." She is one of my greatest joys. I think she looks dashing when she sits, poised high, on a rooftop chimney pot. She is such an agile climber.

Yesterday, Craig and I went for a hike down our country road. Tucked into a haystack nestled down out of the wind with the sun on our faces, we ate a picnic on our own *Casanovalta* land. We harvested chestnuts fallen from our own full-crested tree. Climbing down the hill beside the tree, we found clumps of yellow-brown mushrooms, the same color as the fallen leaves. We are thrilled to be harvesting our first *funghi*. First we will have to ask an Italian to know if they're edible. They resemble a non-edible variety we saw in our *funghi* book. We've heard horror stories about entire local families being wiped out by eating wild mushrooms which turned out to be deadly poison.

When Craig and I returned home to *Casanovalta*, we roasted our precious chestnuts beneath the fireplace embers. They were exceptionally moist and good—probably because they were fresh from the forest floor—and our own. They sent out a rich earthy aroma as they roasted. We are loving the land.

November 5

I enjoyed a day of feeling centered and well—settled and contented in this *Casanovalta* setting. I made a delicious soup on inspiration which contained finely chopped everything; chicken, onion, potato, mushroom, garlic, celery, carrot, parsley, ground nutmeg, etc. etc.— damn good.

Tomorrow Italo, the ironmonger, will come to install the metal dampers in the chimneys but Antonio, our master stone mason, can't help him. He has to work on a rock wall by the back terraces. Last Saturday when Antonio could have worked, Italo wasn't ready. We're also waiting for Rolando, our red-headed plumber from the nearby town of Levane, and Burbui, the furnace man, to come as a team to turn on the radiator system. We've been waiting, and waiting, and waiting.

November 9

Today was a typical day at *Casanovalta*. Our day began with a visit from Rolando, the plumber. Rolando rather resembles a Tuscan troll. He has a shock of red-orange hair, which is typical of a true Tuscan of the region, pale skin with freckles, and a pointed nose. He is from the town of Levane, not far from our town of Pergine. The day before, Craig and I had been forced to eat the wretched food at *La Querce* restaurant as we waited until 9:30 p.m. to talk with Rolando. We pleaded with him, in person, to please come turn on the radiators. We had driven by his house twice before that to leave messages. He took pity on us and agreed to come.

Good to his word he did show up, but we quickly lost confidence in his intelligence. He repeatedly fumbled in his attempt to turn on the radiators to our heating system. It was clear that Burbui's presence was much needed. Burbui is the owner of the local furnace shop and was the technician who had installed our furnace originally—and the malfunctioning radiators. He seemed like a solid and dependable businessman, but he has been letting us down.

Rolando pronounced that the wires were crossed at the thermostat control and in order to have 20 degrees centigrade, we must set the thermostat at 10 degrees centigrade, and so and so on. He didn't bring a wrench, or a screwdriver, and asked, "*Dove sono i tuoi?*" He stated, "Nothing is broken in the system. Burbui claimed a *motorino* (little motor) was broken—but it isn't" and on and on. The whole thing is terribly confusing for me and Craig and we don't feel at all confident that Rolando knows what he is talking about—let alone understands our particular furnace and radiator system.

Awhile later, we were dismayed to observe that the multiple radiators were not very hot and that the temperatures varied among them. No appreciable chill was being taken off the four major rooms of our thick-walled stone and tile house. In fact, I seemed to be made more aware of the cold. I felt growing frustration after experiencing such high hopes for a bit of comfort.

So Craig and I piled into our Fiat, (mud-colored to match the mud in our road so we would never know when it's dirty). We decided to go to Arezzo to face the trucking company. Craig had shipped trunks from California with his blood pressure medicine in them. This presented a problem with customs because you're not allowed to bring medicine into Italy if you can buy it here. We need a certificate from an Italian doctor declaring the content of the pills. After we've done that, then we can arrange another meeting to attempt to get our goods through customs. We now have to explain this hold-up in our best Italian to the truckers.

After meeting with the truckers, we went to the phone company. We want to have a telephone in Italy—at last. There was massive red tape but the phone company officials were friendly and nice. We were assigned a telephone number (89 70 71)—and Craig signed on the dotted line. They will bring the telephone poles from the neighboring town of Pieve a Presciano. This means bringing a single telephone line for many kilometers along a rutted and barely used backcountry dirt road running up a hill and through a forest.

We discussed at length about how to bring the last hundred meters underground in the same canal as the electric. This way we can protect the aesthetic of our country home. A technician will come to our house on Friday to review the situation. It is all set.

Back home at *Casanovalta* we returned to semi-cold radiators, some of them were mildly warm, and others stone cold. We were furious. As promised, Rolando came by to check if the radiators were functioning. We showed him that they were not working.

Rolando, Craig, and I all went below the house to the furnace room to inspect the system and discovered there was a very bad odor. The starter motor within the furnace system, which circulated water to the radiators, was burned out. Rolando was surprised to hear that Burbui had replaced the same burned-out motor just two weeks before.

So here we were back at the beginning—just like the month before—with nothing working. Why in hell didn't Burbui and Rolando come together to our house as they said they would? Why doesn't any worker seem to know his job? We have no heat and it is raining down our chimneys.

November 10 (Sequel to the radiator story)

So, there we were back at the beginning again. I stopped at Burbui's shop in the town of Levane while I was passing through on my way to Montevarchi, the larger town where I do the major part of my household shopping. I was attempting to explain my problem to Burbui's wife, a plump matron with an ample bosom—when who should walk in the shop but Rolando, our miscreant plumber. He had seen me walk in and dared to show his face. The big question on my mind was, "Why had the motor burned up again?"

Rolando suggested, "Perhaps the electrical plant to the house is faulty." Burbui's wife vigorously nodded her head in agreement. "Perhaps the motor was mis-wired. Or, *(best idea of all)* perhaps the motor was struck by lighting!" Burbui's wife really liked that one. I protested that it hadn't rained that day. Rolando rejoined, as though he were pulling a rabbit out of a hat, "Yes, it had rained!" Rolando gallantly volunteered to return to *Casanovalta* to install a new *motorino*—but he cautioned that before we used it, we should have electricians come to the house to double-check the system.

That evening, true to his word, Rolando came to install the new (3rd) *motorino*. I carefully noted that his installation and wiring were opposite from before. I commented on that. He claimed breezily, "Oh, it can go either way." As he started the ignition motor, he checked to make sure water was in it. To our complete joy, all the radiators heated up evenly. They felt toasty.

Not wanting for anything to go wrong again I said, "Well, I guess we better shut off the radiators until the electricians can come by to check out the electrical system." Rolando replied, "Oh, I think it will be all right now." I queried, "No electricians now?" Rolando demurred, "No."

Then he sheepishly asked, on behalf of Burbui, that he be paid for the previous *motorino*. Barbui had forgotten to put it on the bill.

At that juncture, my halting Italian became more fluent. I explained emphatically that we were not keen on paying for three motors until we determined *why had they burned up in the first place?* The plumber suggested we take one of the burned out motors to the manufacturer to ask, "Why?" "*Come mai è brusciato questo motorino?*" (How come this little motor has burned up?)

As a mechanic at the manufacturer told us laughingly the next day, "Motors turn in only one direction to force the water up into the radiators. If they are installed wrong they will force the water down, out of the system, and the motor will burn up at once."

One would think that two men who spend half their lives installing radiator systems would know that. Or perhaps they do know it, but just aren't admitting it.

November 20
Our home on the hill was surrounded by men and dogs on a *caccia al cinghiale* (wild boar hunt) today. The men yelling and dogs baying lasted all day until nightfall. *Casanovalta* is located in the middle of a hunting reserve. The terrible sound of the hunt makes my blood run cold.

November 21
My dog and I went to gather edible chestnuts in the forest. We blended with the golden colors of the fall leaves. While we were gone, my husband, an architect, and the stone mason, the major builder for our house, broke the main water pipe to the radiators. Their bright idea was to let in a bit of heat from the furnace room, which is located below the kitchen. So they drilled a hole in the kitchen floor with the intention of installing a grill—and hit the water pipe. Water gushed out pouring onto the furnace and all over the furnace room. The furnace is now water-logged and will no longer turn on to heat water. We had just repaired it and were enjoying hot water in the bath tub, and in the radiators, for the first time in a long while. Now we are without heat of any kind.

November 23
The plumber has not come to fix the broken water pipe. I'm cold and depressed.

The good news is that we received a telegram inviting us to Rome for a Thanksgiving dinner at the home of Robert and Beverly Katz. What a welcome surprise and diversion. The Katzes are some of our most entertaining Tuscan neighbors. As is fashionable, they have a house in the country and an apartment in Rome. Robert is an American author and screenwriter who wrote the infamous film, *Massacre in Rome*, starring Richard Burton. He has incurred the wrath of the Vatican by accusing Pope Paul XII of failing to act to stave off a Nazi massacre of 335 Italians, including 70 Jews, in 1944. He's currently being sued by the family of the Pope for defaming his memory. The Katz family are doing their best to keep a low profile in Rome these days.

November 24

A dour new plumber came in the morning to solder the copper water pipe. He replaced the punctured part with a new piece. He didn't want to have a thing to do with our systems. He kept a blank face during his entire visit. To all my questions he kept saying in a monotonous nasal voice, *"Non lo so. Non lo so."* (I don't know). True—he didn't know anything. The radiators remained stone cold and the *bruciatore* (furnace) malfunctioned. It would start for a few minutes, heating the water to less than 40°C, then turn itself off never to come on again.

As in the beginning long ago, we can no longer enjoy a hot bath. It is back to heating a pot of water on the stove and taking a sponge bath. As we watch dusk turn into the darkness of night, our spirits sink lower and lower.

November 25

A pleasant diversion today was meeting Sir Joseph Cheyne. He's the regal father of our friend and neighbor, John Cheyne, a willowy and boyish ne'er-do-well fellow who has a shock of brown hair which always falls into his eyes. Sir Joseph is a tall, slender, elegant gentleman from the old school. John was obviously in awe and proud of his distinguished father. John had been the riding master for the eldest daughter of the prestigious local Sistine family and distinguished himself by marrying her, and together they produced a chubby and darling child named Edward. Sir Joseph, John, Craig, and I enjoyed lunch together at *Le Cantine* (The Cellars) our slightly sterile but nicest local Pergine restaurant.

Sir Joseph conversed entertainingly at lunch—after which, we drove the two of them up to Florence. He gave an eloquent lecture at the British Embassy on Keats, Byron, Shelley, and their "Pisan Circle." Sir Joseph, a former diplomat and Romantic poets scholar, is the curator of the esteemed Keats-Shelley Memorial House in Rome, located near the Spanish Steps. I enjoyed the elegance of our day in *Firenze*, the setting, the gentleman, and the occasion.

THANKSGIVING

November 26

Craig and I rushed to catch the 1 p.m. express train to Rome, a two hour trip. After breathlessly arriving on the platform, we received the news that all trains were late. The first train that pulled into the station for Rome was euphemistically called a diretto (direct). Foolishly, we took it—never again. It ambled across the countryside stopping at every little village along the way until it finally chugged into *Roma* at 4:30 p.m.

Thanksgiving dinner, 8 p.m. Roman style at the Katz apartment, was a romp. Craig and I were surrounded by brilliantly comedic novelists, screen writers, and magazine and newspaper columnists. One fellow, Bill Murray, a writer for The New Yorker was particularly droll. He wrote a column titled "From Italy with Love." The men were like fraternity brothers together and kept setting each other up for jokes—and then topping each other with one-liners. I had to hold my sides because they hurt so much from laughing.

My hostess, Beverly Katz, said she was serving the traditional Thanksgiving dinner the way it was always done during her childhood in the Bronx, "Chopped chicken liver, stuffed cabbage, and turkey." Someone quipped, "Yeah, the Indians said, 'Here, have some more stuffed cabbage'." I noticed that the one Italian in our midst carefully avoided the cranberry sauce, yams with orange butter, and shuddered at sight of the pumpkin pie.

November 27

Having just arrived back from Rome today, I sit stoking the fire in the massive kitchen fireplace at *Casanovalta.* Our fireplace is large enough

to cook an entire wild boar. The night air felt warm and misty when I went walking with my dog, "Keshkek." Just a word about our dog—Craig calls him an "American sports dog" because he's a champion frisbee player. Actually, he's a mutt I chose from a litter of puppies, Golden Retriever and terrier mix, because I fell in love with him. We happened to be eating a Yugoslavian slow-cooked chicken and grain dish called "cheshkek"for dinner at our friend's house the night we found him there. Somehow the name seemed to fit—a mixed-up mutt.

November 29

Today, I painted the bathroom wall edging carefully to the wooden ceiling beams with a water color brush. The rough cement wall has to have the paint worked into its irregular, absorbent surface. The finished effect was dazzling. The *muratore* (mason and builder of walls) made only one error today in the upper bathroom, which he has to tear out and re-do tomorrow. I'll make sure of that. I'm a stickler for detail.

Practically all the menfolk from our village of Pergine Valdarno came up the hill today to hunt *cinghiale* (wild boar). They didn't catch any.

Craig turned on the *bruciatore* (furnace i.e. burner) several times during the course of the day—so by nightfall there was enough hot water for a steaming hot tub bath. We also added a pot of boiling water from the stove. Soaking in that tub of hot water was pure bliss.

November 28

Craig and I spent the morning wondering if a repairman would show up to fix the *bruciatore*. He did not.

Craig painted in his art barn all day long. He has a wonderful cast iron wood burning stove in there. It's toasty and serene—and is his sanctuary.

November 31

The radiators are working again. With great drama, Rolando wrenched at water pipes and got soaked to the skin. I stood by, with flashlight in hand, as his plumber's assistant to "*Venga!*" (Come) or, "*Spenga!*" (Shut off the switch). He called out these commands as I jumped to follow his orders. He replaced a control device that was automatic but calcified from the great quantity of calcium in our water. Now, we will have to open and shut the waterline to our radiators manually about every ten days until a dial on a pressure gauge reaches a certain point. It's a bit nerve wracking—but I'm happy to do it for the pleasure of hot water. I have no idea what Rolando did to fix the *bruciatore*, but the thermostat now registers 60°C. I went up to the kitchen to dry my feet at the fireplace.

Craig and I are so grateful to be warm we have decided to leave the radiators on all night. I have my third sore throat and cold of the season.

As a postscript to the hot water saga, Craig had a tense moment this evening when he went to draw his bath and no water came out of the tap. The plumber had forgotten to turn the *autoclave* (pressure pump) back on. Craig turned on the *autoclave* and water was able to rise to the third floor bathroom. Craig could have a hot bath. We both heaved a sigh of relief.

Winter

December 2

Yet another starving hunting dog has found its way to our doorstep. Craig fed it four times and put it in a basket in our furnace room to get dry and warm. This has become our ritual of kindness. The bony dog is in much better shape than the last poor little dog. A few weeks ago, we had a very sick bitch with a large tumor put to sleep at the veterinarian's office, after we got her warm and fed. We wanted her passing to be gentle. We just couldn't keep her. The responsibility felt like the last straw to our ability to cope. But we're haunted by the memory of how happy she was to ride in the car going to the vet. Of course, she didn't know she was on her way to her doom. She kept trying to lift her head up to see out of filmed eyes as she rode—but then kept drifting off to sleep, her head nodding between us. Craig and I felt sad about her. We would have kept her if we had not brought Keshkek, our Golden Retriever/terrier mutt, from California to Italy. We felt that Keshkek was a full time job and we just couldn't care for two dogs. For this most recent dog, we'll post the news in Pergine and tell the hunting society.

Our wonderful new radiators have only one flaw—we can't control the heat. They're either on—full boar, or off—stone cold. The thermostats are wall ornaments. We have to go to the furnace room to flip the switches "on" or "off." Last night, we thought that we had the thermostats set on "low"—(in reverse, of course), and sweltered in the heat as they blasted away all night. We're very grateful for the heat, but I was a sweaty lump by morning. We asked the plumber if there was any particular reason he could think of as to why Burbui would not come to our house to *sistemare* (adjust) the thermostats? The plumber said he thought that Burbui, the furnace man, would come. Tonight we have the burner/furnace turned "Off."

December 6

I just enjoyed a magical romp in enchanting *Firenze* with my girlfriend, Sheila, who blew into town for three days. We talked until the wee hours, laughed, and shopped while hanging onto each other's arm. She bought out Celine, an exclusive boutique where she had always shopped as a Pan Am stewardess—and I got my hair cut.

We discovered a hidden garden selling antiques on *Via S. S. Apostoli*. Within the garden walls was a charming garden house with its own tiny front yard in the heart of *Firenze*. I liked experiencing bustling early-morning *Firenze*, and twilight *Firenze*, with its newly strung Christmas lights twinkling across the passageways. My joie de vivre was given breath.

An amusing, (but also pathetic), anecdote is that when I opened my suitcase in Sheila's room at the Excelsior, a puff of smoke almost billowed out. My clothes reeked of fireplace smoke.

Back home in the country, Craig and I worked all day Sunday on the house with the mason. I had a hacking cough, as my cold had gotten worse. Today, we're attempting to clean up the fine cement dust and general mess. Craig worked really hard, and I sacrificed keeping my ribs in place. Keshkek finally got a bath. The firewood was delivered at last—and Craig stacked it all.

CHRISTMAS

December 19

It's snowing at *Casanovalta*, the first snow of the winter. We really will be having a white Christmas. Christmas music is filling the house, American music from a tape we bought in Florence. We also saw an American movie in Florence on Friday night. Our cup has been full lately. Craig, a Southern California boy, is so excited to be experiencing his first white Christmas—highlighted by its being at *Casanovalta*.

The zest of the season, and the antique quality of Florence, blended in the sights and sounds of street musicians from *Abruzzo* playing homemade bagpipes and looking for holiday handouts. *Abruzzo* is an Italian state which is quite mountainous in the western part and has a more challenging existence. *"Forte e gentile"* (strong and gentle) best describes the beauty of the region and the character of its people. Our stone mason, Antonio, is from that region. I think the men are especially handsome too, many with their raven black hair, dense eyebrows, and penetrating eyes.

A file of children followed a "parade of one" as a bagpiper padded down *Via Porta Rossa* (road of the red door) stepping into each shop on his lucrative musical journey. It was like a reenactment of the "Pied Piper of Hamlin." Our favorite little hotel in Florence is the *Albergo Porta Rossa.* We could see the musician as we poked our heads out of our window facing onto the narrow street. The street was festooned with green leafy garlands—and the festive sights of Florence at Christmastime lay below us.

At night in the main *piazze* (squares), young looking Santa Clauses (*San Nicola)* led tiny, snowy-white island ponies for young children to get a Christmas ride. One man was playing a calliope with his Pekingese dog on top. His wife was passing out prayer cards to donors.

Our jolly Christmas visit to Florence was topped off by finding a shop serving proper Viennese hot dogs—good bun, mustard, onions, and sauerkraut—as served in the streets of New York City (or Vienna). We gobbled one down on the way to a movie—blissed out. As we returned to the hotel after the movie, we delighted in the Christmas lights and enormous trees in each piazza—truly festive.

Re: central heating—I had a toe to toe debate with Burbui re: the burned out little motors and his part in it. I don't know if I lost the debate—but I feel grievance over three burned out motors. I needed to express that.

Craig and I are cleaning the house for our Christmas party, which will be a gracious affair. It is our first Christmas at *Casanovalta*.

December 27

At the moment, I'm riding on an Italian train on my way to Austria. This feels like the perfect time to describe the joys of Christmas in *Italia*.

The festival season here is far more beautiful than in California. The brisk air adds to the sense of vivacity. All the towns are delightful with their decorated trees and lights. However, the queen in her splendor is *Firenze*. Craig and I went there again for last minute Christmas Eve shopping. The Florentines were coiffed, cloaked, and gowned for Christmas Eve. With recently purchased gifts in hand, they were headed out for gala dinners with friends. We sipped our *caffè Hag con crema* (instant decaffeinated coffee with cream) at Gilli's Cafe and absorbed the glamor of the "beautiful people" as they sipped green or pink colored cocktails from slender crystal goblets. They postured elegantly at the bar with their cigarettes. I felt as though I was watching a play.

Christmas day was a phenomenon. It began with *pranzo in famiglia* (family lunch) at the Peruzzi's home in Montevarchi. Craig had befriended the head of the Italian Electric Company, ENEL, in our area so we received the honor of being welcomed into the bosom of their family, which included Signor Peruzzi's handsome elderly parents. I felt they were the salt of the earth.

However, we disgraced ourselves by arriving late for this formal occasion. Craig had somehow not been clear on the exact time we should arrive. We had even eaten a bite of breakfast before going—which proved to be a huge mistake. The entire Peruzzi family had risen at the crack of dawn to prepare the feast and were waiting for us attired in their Sunday best, with barely concealed outrage. Craig and I poured on the charm and were eventually able to make them smile.

In honor of the occasion, the table was set with a hand-embroidered tablecloth and cloth napkins. A display of *crostini* (little toasts), *prosciutto* (dried ham), and pickled vegetables were already in place. These were followed by *raviolini in brodo* (little ravioli in broth), boiled *capon* (castrated young rooster)—which the grandmother coyly claimed to have castrated herself—and *zampone* (a seasonal type of boiled pork sausage), and potato puree. Our eyes bugged out when that offering was followed by the roasted meat course; *faraona* (guinea hen), *piccione* (pigeon), and pork-roast.

Green salad was presented as a digestive course so we all could enjoy the cornucopia of desserts which followed. The *dolci* (confectionary) consisted of *budino* (vanilla pudding), *panforte* (traditional Sienese fruitcake), *pandolce* (sweet Christmas bread), marzipan candies, and almond cookies to dip in wine, accompanied by a mountain of fruit; sliced fresh pineapple, tangerines, and grapes. Of course, the entire repast was washed down with liters of *Chianti, Vinsanto* (Italian sherry), and finally, *Spumante* (sparkling wine)—followed by coffee.

Craig and I did our heroic best to show our appreciation by eating as much as we could hold—and carrying-on in our best Italian. We were absolutely stuffed and in pure awe of the effort put forth by the entire Peruzzi family.

To have a complete Christmas Day, we went visiting in the late afternoon to call on Osvaldo at *Cennina*. He was delighted to see us. His fortunes have gone very badly. He and his brother have cancer. This is sad because they are both remarkable and unique men—so talented, creative, and adventurous.

My journal thoughts are interrupted by conversations on the train. Travelers in my compartment were saying, *"Cortina d'Ampezzo is lovely. San Martino di Castrozza...montagne, boschi meravigliosi"* (the mountains and forests are marvelous). *"Le Pale di San Martino, il cinanon del Pala*

Sasso—un gruppo di montagne bellissimi!" (a group of beautiful mountains).

In the evening, Craig and I finished off Christmas Day with a visit to the Zaccheo family who were having a Swedish Christmas planned by Ugo Zaccheo's Swedish wife, Kajsa. Actually, we got what was left of one because Ugo was not clear about the time. We tasted the remains of Kajsa's famous, labor intensive, chestnut cake—Ugo's favorite. (He ate most of it).

On the Wednesday before Christmas, Craig and I hosted a grand party where we blended local Italian friends with our *stranieri* (foreigner) friends. Our famous punch, (actually it is my secret wine punch recipe originally from *Gourmet* Magazine), was a great equalizer. *Stranieri* and locals discovered that they could converse together quite well. We truly gave a magical party full of rustic charm and holiday flavors. *Casanovalta* glowed in candlelight with its windows and arches decked out with evergreen boughs. At the end of the evening, Craig and I both felt overwhelmed by Italian generosity and goodwill.

December 30

"Ich bin schiffen in Austria!" (I've been skiing in Austria). I believe you can judge a country by its coffee—and that makes Austria tops. I truly enjoyed the coffee and the *schnee* (snow). I found the countryside big and grand, and the houses pretty, large, and sparkling clean. The air was sharp and fresh—healthy. It snowed in the evening of both days I was in St. Martin. I was enjoying cross-country skiing in the heart of *Salzburgerland* , which is the scenic countryside outlying the city of Salzburg. This was a remarkably special time being with my sister, Brenda, and her husband, Axel Ahrens.

Coming back to Italy, I have the impression of a higher density of people living in cement box apartment buildings, multi-family dwellings that are stark and similar. In Northern Italy, my eyes see more civilization and less charm—once again, the sloppy Italian jumble. But the Italians are gregarious and somehow get on with life.

∽ *1983* ∽

THE NEW YEAR

January 3

Italy wears thin on me when the electric company turns off all electricity for three hours in the morning until midday, 11 a.m. until 2 p.m., without any warning. I think it's an invasion of personal rights. This is what it does to my hair washing. 1) I'm cold because I can't turn on the electric heater. 2) There is no water pressure because the *autoclave* (water pump) can't function. 3) Eventually, there is no hot water because the furnace cannot turn on. 4) Lastly, there is no water because the *autoclave* isn't working to lift it to the second floor. 5) So then, I can't even rinse the soap out of my hair and I'm shivering in a scarcely-filled tub. 6) And the final blow is that I can't even dry my hair because my electric hair dryer won't work. So, I'm sitting around in the dead of winter with a wet head. 7) And the house is getting colder and colder because the furnace isn't heating the water for the radiators.

Hooray—the electricity just came on—the workers have gone home for *pranzo* (lunch).

January 4

I'm sick in bed with my fourth cold of the winter—which I find very discouraging. The cloud that sits on this house most of the time makes me feel like I'm in an isolation ward. Craig and I plan to take a drive to the Amalfi Coast soon.

January 5

I lay in bed today with a raging fever. Craig kindly let me spend the day in his big bed in the warmer, dryer bedroom. I can look out the window and see a tree—not a big enveloping cloud like seen out my bedroom window. My bedroom is in the back of the house with a window that faces towards the valley below. My little bed is tucked beside a stone staircase which leads to our upper bathroom. Wind blows under the bathroom door and over my bed in a drafty manner all night long.

I'm very sick, vacillating between being chilled or feverish. I want to go home to my mommy and daddy in Laguna Beach for the cure, parental nurturing, and sun. Craig and I laughed over the classic line from the movie *E.T.*, "E.T. phone home!" Craig applied it to my current situation saying, "Ani phone home!" He has more than held his end up by being cheerful and taking good care of me. I feel profoundly cut off from external stimulus.

January 6

This was certainly a "day in the life." Craig and I had to go to Arezzo to get our *permessi di soggiorno* (residence permits)—as we were overdue already. Our village of Pergine Valdarno is located within the Provence of Arezzo. We should have had them before Christmas—but nobody knew where we were supposed to go to get them. Arezzo "police information" sent us to the wrong place—after we had gone to the original wrong place suggested by the Pergine police. By the time we figured out where to go, everyone had closed for lunch. So today, we headed straight for the *Palazzo del Governo* (Government Palace).

The only trouble with Italy, among the many, is that urban planners forgot to include places to park your car—especially near important public buildings. Italians were double parked in every crevice available. We chose a reasonable place, in a line of other cars which were already parked between two signs that indicated NO PARKING. We felt lucky to find the spot.

Inside the *Palazzo del Governo*, we went to the office marked *stranieri* (foreigners) and tried to do business with a lady who impatiently jabbered away at us as though she thought we were native born. I wondered what she was doing working in the *stranieri* office?

No one had mentioned to us previously that we needed to go to the tobacco shop to buy two official sheets of paper with government stamps on them. So Craig and I walked to a tobacco shop—where they were out of official stamps. So then, we had to walk in search of another tobacco shop. By then, I was getting all weak and sweaty because I had just arisen from a sick bed to do this official business. When we finally returned to the *Palazzo di Governo*, my temper was on a short tether. So when the older woman in the office rapidly spewed a technical sentence at me, I snapped, "*Non ho capito una parola!*" *Parla più lentamente!*" (I have not understood a word. Speak more slowly). She did settle down a notch or two after that. Craig and I signed our names for the *permessi* (permits)—and then only needed to get a photocopy of the deed to our house to give to our local police in Pergine. That meant we would have to track down a certain long lost lawyer—but that would be another day. So, we gratefully walked back to our car to find that it—complete with a dog inside—was missing.

I flagged down a passing police car and told the officer that our car was missing. He told us to go to the *Questura* (police headquarters). That was where we had just been. At the Questura, they told us to go to "police information" by the train station. So we walked there—speculating all the while that our car had been towed away, that everything would close for lunch, and we'd be trapped in Arezzo all day. The police officer verified that our car had indeed been towed—just twenty minutes earlier, the length of time it had taken us to find the government stamps.

Neither Craig nor I could remember our license plate number, which annoyed the policeman—but the identifying mark was that our car had a dog inside. The policeman called the garage and asked them not to close for lunch until we got there. We took a taxi from the train station to the car pound. We found the car—and Keshkek, looking not too disturbed. The tow charge and ticket only came to 27,000 lire. So, apropos of the moment, we went to see the movie "E.T."—dubbed in Italian. My eyes filled with tears when I heard the dear little extraterrestrial utter the immortal lines, "*E. T. telefono casa!*" (E.T. phone home).

January 7

I think my main lesson to date has been learning how to cope with life in a foreign country. In Austria, Vermont, or the California High Sierras, winter is beautiful and gleaming like an icicle. It is snowy, flaky, and exciting. In Italy, so far, it has been a void —*niente*—an in-between space that is nothing.

This is my insightful thought: Taoists believe a void will be filled— each polar opposite contains the seed of the other—which means there is hope.

January 11

I was right—the balance has tipped towards a sense of well-being. Yesterday, the sun was penetratingly bright. This condition followed winds that howled around the house the night before. In celebration, Keshkek and I went on an exuberant walk to re-visit our favorite places. We could see hills beyond hills and distant snow-capped mountains. Blades of grass were distinct, and each small hill-town was sharply defined in silhouette, side-lit. "Keshy" and I found a clump of heavy budded winter flowers. I sensed that we both felt the promise of hope— and spring.

January 16

Craig and I took time off to visit an enchanted land—Ravello. One thousand feet straight up from sea level, this town, loved by anyone who has ever lived or visited here, gazes out over lemon tree covered terraced hills which stretch down to the Tyrrhenian Sea. The streets are narrow Roman footpaths with stone walls covered in moss, ferns, and violets—

the grey rocks softened by antiquity. The Villa Rufolo and the Villa Cimbrone, with their formal gardens and panoramic views, reflect the influence of the Romans, Moors, and Normans.

Flowers grow everywhere peeping out of nooks and crevices, and cascading over terraced walls. Wagner visited the Villa Rufolo at the time he was composing his opera, *Parsifal*, and wrote in the guest book on May 26, 1880, "The enchanted garden of Klingsor has been found!" I share his passion.

January 22

Back home in Tuscany, Craig and I went to a chamber music concert in Siena sponsored by the *Academia Chigiana* at the *Pallazzo Chigi*. This evening was a rare experience which feels like what living in Europe should be all about. Siena seemed its most medieval and mystical self, lit by nighttime illumination. We took the passageways and steep steps which lead to, and suddenly open upon, the magnificent *Piazza del Campo*. We wanted to eat our pre-concert pizza at one of the little restaurants located there.

From there, a short walk took us to the freshly painted Baroque splendor of the concert hall. I liked the mixture of students and fur-clad matrons in the audience. The violin soloist and her father, the piano accompanist, appeared at first to be concert puppets carved from wood. He was white with age and strode stiffly onto the stage. His daughter rose onto her toes during the lyrical passages with her long, mousy hair falling across her cheeks. But their dedication and virtuosity as musicians was very much alive, and I was soon carried away with the joy of it.

One of the most satisfying moments occurred during the encore when the old gentleman's face, flush with the success of the evening, softened into a smile. He and his daughter had done well.

January 23

After drinking too much wine and eating too much garlic, I reminded myself again of Taoism and the need to maintain balance between mundane and spiritual things. No extreme is good—as it invites its opposite for balance.

January 25

This is one of those delirious sort of days when our world is deliciously sunny on our hilltop while the valley below is covered in clouds, fog, and mist. Arezzo is chilled, icy, and shrouded in hoar frost. It is an inversion of our normal condition.

Craig and I put our most persuasive foot forward at the phone company, SIP, to convince them not to destroy our nature walk with telephone poles. They want to do it their way—conserving the natural beauty of the landscape does not concern them much. But there is a glimmer of hope, and we'll keep fighting. They'll be sending up a second technician—or the same technician a second time.

We were delighted to return to our sun spot. I sat on our rear terrace wall and gazed out over the distant hills—*un po di calma* (a little bit of calm). Keshkek and Muffin shared the peace of the moment with me.

January 26

I think I should stop worrying about what my next step will be, and just know that there is a next step. I must have faith that I will know—or can figure out—what the next step will be when I come to it.

January 28

Tonight, Craig and I are going to Florence to see a Woody Allen movie and eat hot dogs. Yay.

January 29

The *muratore* (mason) bashed about in the house all day.

February 2

I have passed through another rugged period. Just when I was feeling well and hopeful for spring to be here before too long, Craig got struck down by influenza with its dreadful side effects.

Then I got gripped at the throat by what feels like an insidious lizard, all scales and claws. The last two days have looked very black.

Today unfolded rather spontaneously. I went to find the village doctor for us—and inquired at the post office. Sweetly, the post mistress had one of the delivery men drive me over to the doctor's house. He explained solicitously to the doctor's wife that the architect at *Casanovalta* had need of a doctor because he had the flu. The doctor's wife said the doctor would come to our house as soon as possible. I find it rather charming to be in a foreign land where the country doctor still makes house calls.

From there, I went to do business at the bank in Ambra where I exchanged pleasantries with the bankers, and afterwards stopped by Jeffrey Smart's house with various messages. He invited me to stay for lunch, which tasted so good and nourishing. I loved sitting on his sun-filled *loggia* (second story open to the air living area) with his charming canaries warbling away and the tropical plants bursting with new growth in the warmth and sunlight of that happy spot.

Jeffrey Smart, who describes himself as a "poofter," is an acclaimed Australian painter of the photorealism genre. He lives full time in Italy making infrequent trips to Australia. His art studio is in a cozy stone structure separate from his large and gracious home in Pieve a Presciano. One of his major works hangs in the Melbourne Opera House. It is an enormous mural showing a train, with multi-colored cars, moving through a eucalyptus forest.

Jeffrey and his young and handsome partner, Ermes de Zan, seem so content in their home. I felt inspired by their lunch preparations—although Jeffrey bellowed at Ermes, "Peel the fucking potatoes!" To which Ermes grumbled, "OK, I'll peel the fucking potatoes." We enjoyed a lively conversation at the midday meal. Then I returned home to the sickness and the depression. Craig has not felt like painting for many months. He quipped, "I painted my canvas black."

I expressed the idea to Craig that "he didn't need to make a living from painting—but he needed to paint to live."

February 3

The dapper doctor came to call for a meager 10,000 Lire. There was nothing to be done for our virus infections except live through them. He did prescribe a medicine which had live microbes living on a yeast substance in a vial. They were the "good guys" which were supposed to go to work in Craig's intestine. Ironically, the doctor had the same throat. He spoke in the same raspy voice as my own. We both agreed that we couldn't sleep at night with the discomfort. Our Pergine doctor very much admired *Casanovalta* and what we'd done to restore it.

February 6
This is beginning to feel like the "Diary of a Mad Woman." It could be a good psychological study of what happens to someone who is living on a hilltop, in the middle of a forest, in a country where you don't speak the language, and you don't have a telephone, TV, or any other connection with the outside world. The weather is consistently cold, grey, and damp—and you are constantly ill with respiratory diseases. And on top of that, the relationship with your only companion is starting to disintegrate—no small wonder on that score.

February 8
Our Tuscan country neighbors, Ugo and Kajsa Zaccheo, have invited me as their guest to take a ski vacation in the *Dolomiti* (Dolomites), in the region of *Anterselva di Sopra* (the forest above). There is also *Anterselva di Sotto,* (the forest below)—and we will cross-country ski from one to the other gliding down the mountain, from *Sopra* to *Sotto.* I will be taking a break from my routine.

Ugo and Kajsa are a unique couple. Ugo Zaccheo is an elegant Italian who as a boy had attended an elite Catholic school run by French priests near the Spanish Steps in Rome and speaks English with a British accent. He was a former director of Alitalia Airlines. He withdrew from that position to retire to Tuscany with his wife, Kajsa, where he had inherited the estate *"La Fornace"* outside of Badia Agnano from his father. There they are cultivating vineyards and olive groves. Their son is attending Cornell University and their daughter Princeton in the United States. Although the son protests, "I'm not majoring in the United States!"

Ugo tells the story about riding to Sweden on his motor bike as a young man, with a buddy. They were in pursuit of beautiful blonde Swedish girlfriends. He met Kajsa, who was working in a chemist's shop, and won her over with his suave charm and brilliant smile. She fell for him, and now she's stuck with a self-absorbed Italian husband. He did give her a large wooden loom for weaving tapestries, which is set up in its own room at *La Fornace*. Kajsa is a talented tapestry artist, among all her other strengths and gifts.

Here in *Anterselva di Sopra,* the 1983 World Cup Biathlon competition is going to be held in one week. That means all the international teams are here—lean and fleet with their rifles slung across their backs. Here I am, shuffling along the tracks in my Nordic skis, when I hear the rush of wind and the slick glide of racing skis on icy snow as brilliantly clad young athletes fly past me. It is absolutely thrilling. I try to imitate their stride and arm movements for a pace or two—then quit. I think admiringly, "Poetry in motion —what robustness—how beautiful to watch."

February 10

"Home, home on the range," I sing to myself. Ah, now for a bit of peace and quiet in the country. Another day unfolds at *Casanovalta*, as on my first morning home, I awaken to soft snow falling and notice that outside my covers the bedroom seems quite cold. This is because the *bruciatore* is not working—because paraffin has formed in the *gasolio* due to the cold. The furnace man had just been up to the house to clean the paraffin out of the furnace two days before and gave Craig solvent to put in the *gasolio* tank. Craig hadn't done it yet because the weather was too rainy. He was going to do it today—but the *bruciatore* has become blocked again before he could manage to put it in. Craig has gone out now into the snow to put solvent into the *gasolio* tank. We wondered why no one—for instance Burbui, the furnace man—didn't tell us in advance to put solvent in the *gasolio* tank, such as one might put anti-freeze in the automobile tank. Why wait until paraffin forms and you lose your heat in the middle of a snow storm—when you're just recuperating from the flu—to put solvent into the *gasolio* tank?

So Craig and I begin our day with no furnace making heat for the radiators, and our firewood stack reduced to three pieces. We've been asking our woodman to deliver more wood every week for a month. He would faithfully promise that he would come the following Monday. That Monday never came. So I wrote a note to him crying, "Help! Help!"—and his men did bring up a load in the snow by tractor. Craig and I stacked firewood in the snow until our hands and feet got too cold and wet.

During lunch preparation, ENEL turned off our electricity for an hour or so. This eliminated the extra bit of heat from my electric heater and plunged us into gloom. I hope the electricity doesn't go off in the night because I'm counting on my electric blanket.

Revitalized from my ski vacation, I don't feel too depressed from this typical brand of torture. But poor Craig has been coping the entire time I was gone. He had to crawl up the hill on his hands and knees in the midst of a blizzard Saturday night because the car couldn't climb the last steep bend in the road without snow tires. He also had to get the furnace repaired when it clogged up with paraffin. He really is in no mood to continue suffering in this fashion. But of course we must—and with the best spirit possible. I think we have been extremely good sports over all.

Craig and I ended our evening with a serious discussion about selling *Casanovalta*. We agreed it was the only thing to do because our life here is not what we imagined it would be. This makes eight years of my life feel misdirected.

February 11

Snowbound—piles and piles of snow. It's been snowing so furiously that Craig couldn't get the car out of the driveway to go to the post office. All morning we've been watching snow blowing and billowing around the eves of our stone house and carpeting the high meadow.

In the afternoon sunlight, Keshkek and I ventured out into the virgin mounds of white. His doggy prints pepper the deep, white path of our favorite forest walk to *Campiano*, the nearest abandoned farmhouse. The sheltering tree limbs are laced with white. The distant yet near *Pratomagno* mountains are capped in white. My Angora cat, Muffin, looks yellow against the white as she joins us in the great outdoors. We all celebrate the shimmering white, white world. I yearn with all the strength of my child-heart for a sled, or cross-country skis to glide down our country road.

After multiple passes, Craig managed to jockey our Fiat up to the top of our driveway. From there it is a steep curve down our precipitous exit road. We decided to test our ability to get off our mountain and down to the village. The villagers greeted us warmly—congratulating us for getting down the hill. *"Bravo! Bravo!"* The local talk at Francesca's bar was all about the snow.

Shopping hurriedly for provisions, we decided we better get back before nightfall. This was wise because our access road is too steep at the last part for our snow tires to grip it. We parked the car with the nose pointing downwards, and scrambled up the snow-powdered hill on foot as dark thickened in the forest.

Our home, lit by candlelight and fireplace-glow, felt cozy and warm as we grilled our evening meal of pork chops, seasoned with garlic and rosemary, over the kitchen fire—(actually over charcoals pulled forward onto the hearthstone). Craig and I agreed contentedly that our hill-top retreat was far more scenic than the snow-slush setting of the timid souls down on the flat.

The wind is howling around the house causing kitty to glance up with a worried expression.

February 12

Casanovalta takes on a new warmth when it's covered over in snow. The kitchen fireplace, eternally burning, is the hearth-heart of our home. I'm surprised at how comfortable it has kept us. Other rooms, of course, are icy. All this beauty is in direct contrast to the months upon months of grey that preceded it.

I just had a lovely experience in the *here* and *now*. Because the furnace is not working we have no hot water. So in order to wash my hair, I have to heat water on the stove and dunk my head in the kitchen sink. The kitchen is the warm room. The sunlight streaming through the window, the many colored shades of wood in the wooden countertops, and the steamy water with vapor rising, combine to create the effect of a Swedish sauna or bathhouse—most delightful.

My enjoyment of the moment feels better than worrying, worrying, worrying.

Sometimes I like being far removed from everyone and everything. With us covered over in snow on this hill, no one can get up the road to our house. I think, "Good—no one can come here today. We won't be disturbed."

I ruminate, "The Zaccheos may achieve much more than I do, but they are also much more tense." I felt relief to leave them after our ski vacation and return to the comfort of my own gentle rhythm. I don't like the feeling of them standing in judgment of me—I'm hard enough on myself. (It's amazing how much easier it is to theorize about what I should do—as compared to doing what I should do).

Well, all my harsh thoughts towards my neighbors have melted away. Ugo Zaccheo just walked up our hill, fighting his way though snow at the end of a long day's drive home from Bolzano. Kajsa told him, "Go, go!" Jeffrey Smart told him, "Carry up bread and milk!" Our neighbors were worried about us.

Ugo urged us to ride down with him in his car, parked way down the road. He had carried up my fur-lined rubber boots, which I had forgotten from the ski vacation. He said if it snowed again he would come up by tractor and take us out. Craig and I felt very touched.

February 13

I awoke in the early morning feeling cold. So I thought, "I think I'll turn up my electric blanket." Wrong. The little red light on the dial was out—no electric power. The snow has fallen heavily, and now we are without a furnace or electricity. For the first time, we made positive use of the fireplace in my bedroom. Pachebel's "Canon in D" is playing on the battery operated cassette player, two fireplaces are roaring, candles are burning, and outside is a mantle of white. We are happy—but too much smoke.

Although this day started out cheerfully enough, the isolation and boredom closes in as it wears on. Sleety rain has been falling on the snow. The condition alternates between snow and rain, hence making sleet. I've crawled into bed in my room feeling rather fuzzy from inhaling too much smoke.

I keep getting up to put logs on the fire. My nose is constantly running from the smoke. We are suffering and no longer happy.

The electricity came on in the afternoon—but now there is thunder and lightning—so we may lose it again. Drats. Tomorrow, Craig and I will go down off this hill.

February 15

Despondent. Our smoke-filled world is dreary. Burbui has not come yet to repair the furnace—and I have a constantly flowing head cold. Ugo Zaccheo came up our hill by tractor yesterday, but we had already managed to go down by car. We walked down the steep part of our road on foot, our toes getting frosty inside our boots.

Craig and I were greeted warmly by the staff at Hotel Ambra. They have been consistently sweet to us. We had a polenta lunch and did some shopping for necessities in Pergine. I have been trying to keep up our spirits by cooking yummy cakes and cookies—as eating is one of our only sources of pleasure. I'm sure the draft sweeping across me as I sleep, from the crack under the bathroom door, is unhealthy. Our cold, wet, drafty stone house feels grossly unhealthy.

Craig just struggled back from the post office—(the daily big event in our lives)—with a package full of presents and a long letter from my dear friend, Sheila. Never was a letter from home more appreciated. I huddled by the kitchen fire, attired in my night dress and sweat shirt with a hanky wadded in my pocket, and savored every word. I handed each page to Craig as I was finished. I anointed my grubby body with the perfume she sent and tried to sniff it through my clogged nose. Sheila has been feeling listless. We fully sympathized. I forgave myself some for being so fragile when I observed that even my energetic girlfriend, who I admire greatly, has low periods sometimes. I feel confident now that Craig and I will rally.

Wrong. Kajsa just hiked up the hill to tell us that she had spoken with Burbui's wife—who had a message to give the Ellwoods. "There is nothing more that Burbui can do to repair your heating system. It is up to the man who installed it to clean it out"—that meant our ex-plumber, Pippo. Pippo would have to clean out the lines that come from the *gasolio* tank to the furnace.

Here are my burning questions:
- Why did Burbui wait for one week to give us this information?
- Why didn't Burbui ask Rolando, our current plumber, to come up to clean the lines? He sees Rolando every day, and Burbui knows full well that we no longer use Pippo. Burbui also knows we don't have a phone. And if he knew we needed a plumber, why didn't he speak to our plumber?

As it is, he feels no guilt at leaving us without heat for one week in the middle of a snowstorm. Now, we have to go through the very painful and laborious process of coercing a lying, cheating plumber to come to our house.

In all fairness, I must say I think more highly of our plumber, Rolando, now. He came up our hill on foot with his tools in the icy cold and fixed our furnace. It's my secret thought that his father encouraged him to go right away. But for whatever reason, Rolando did come—and I'm extremely grateful. I just washed a pile of dirty dishes with hot tap water.

I stayed up later than I wanted to attempting to call Muffin in out of the freezing cold, gusty night. I had just given up and was placing a sleeping box for her beside the front door when she came. I had been madly ringing the ship's bell we'd been given as a housewarming present. I had not taken it out of the plastic wrap until this moment—but my throat was raw from calling. It worked very well. Ah, now I get to go to bed in a warmer than usual bedroom—tomorrow Florence.

February 16

Craig awoke in a cheery mood ready to go to Florence. That was a great relief because I worried that he might have caught pneumonia from trudging down and up our hill in the sub-zero temperature after taking a hot bath yesterday. That didn't happen—(he only had an attack of apoplexy).

I feel feeble this morning from my terrible cold, but I'm sure the "Florence-going spirit" will soon spread over me. Clearly, the way to live comfortably in Europe is to be very rich and live in a beautiful city during the winter—then go to your country home during the hot summer months. Anyone who can afford to does it that way—and now I know why.

It amuses me to be all nicely dressed for Florence—and then finish the costume off by putting on chunky rubber boots to walk down the hill. Craig plans to roll up the pant legs of his dress pants. I think we're spunky and gallant.

February 18

Carrying our suitcases up the hill through the ice and snow, we returned from Florence to a re-blocked heating system. The copper tubing the plumber installed above ground will have to be done again and thickly insulated. When the plumber did the original work during the early restoration of the house, he should have installed the pipes way underground—below the freezing level. But the work had been done in a typically incompetent fashion. It should be noted that in Sweden and Austria houses are heated with a consistent supply of heat all winter long. The *gasolio* does not freeze in the lines.

By contrast, Florence was a pageant of vivacious and chicly clad people. Our *pensione* was pleasant and warm, brightly sunlit and spacious—but not as elegant as I had expected from Sheila's description.

We were, nevertheless, comfortable. The movie Craig and I went to was a twisted, foolish tale about three women who had, in one form or another, lost their grip on reality. That was the last movie on earth we needed to see. It depressed us terribly. But the next morning, we felt the energy of the city effect us like a "picker-upper."

I went to the hairdresser as a special treat, but was shocked when the owner of the salon cut my bangs off too short. I felt like I looked awful— like the way I looked when my mother cut my bangs for my ugly "Buster Brown" hairdo in the second grade. Craig said it was all right.

We enjoyed an exquisite lunch at *Lume di Candele* (Candlelight). We blissed out on avocados—very ripe, from Israel—*tasty tortelli di patate,* and finally half-melons from Spain filled with port. Then we went to an art exhibit at the Pitti Palace.

Refreshed, we returned home to greet new misery. However we felt comforted by the Zaccheos, who invited us over to dine with them. The Zaccheos invited us, Jeffrey Smart, and other dinner guests who were Swedish, over for a formal dinner. The Swedes were refined and spoke in extremely soft voices—which I understood was a part of their cultural characteristic. Jeffery however, an outspoken Australian, started speaking louder and louder in an effort to draw them out. So by the end of the evening, it sounded like he was yelling at them. The Swedes only cringed inwardly and spoke even more softly. I thought that if everyone would just lower their voices, we could all hear them.

We blathered on about our problems. Jeffery seemed flip, and I felt annoyed by him. Craig sat there looking forlorn with black gauges under his eyes and his nose dripping gently.

Another major crisis we're coping with is the chaos created by the encroachment of the Algerian Pipe Line. Or as they call it familiarly in Italy, *"La Pipalinea."* The Italian government is bringing oil for Italy all the way from Algeria, by means of an underground pipeline which travels under the Mediterranean Sea. It has come all that way to directly cross the entry road to our property. It intersects our driveway.

The Zaccheos helped us write letters to tie onto the tractor that is digging the trench for the Algerian Pipe Line. We couldn't believe that they'd dug a deep trench across our entry road while we were in Florence. By driving across the earth ridges around the end of the trench, we managed to get back home again. We want them to provide access to our road with a metal plank, or something.

The Algerian Pipe Line is also cutting a wide swath through our local forest, tearing up the Montelucci road, and generally disfiguring the countryside. This has been an underlying theme, adding to the rest of our gloomy outlook. It has been an additional burden, inconvenience, eyesore, and heartache.

I've decided that part of the problem of what's wrong around here is *me*. I'll see what I can do to clean up my act.

A sweet letter from my sister, Brenda, arrived today. She was refused a German government grant to support work on her doctorate in the field of "Open Air Space Planning." She's at a low in her life, yet tries really hard—it seems to me. I think I'll try my best to do better too.

February 19

God must be playing a cat and mouse game, just like my Muffin, with us mortals. He tests us to the breaking point and then—rewards us with a pretty day. Today is dazzling, sunny and happy. 5°C feels absolutely toasty.

I walked to a high point in our yard and gazed at the valley below, and at the distant snow covered *Pratomagno* mountains. I felt reluctant to leave the spot. My heart was bursting with joy. I stood and communed with nature.

I'm sitting on a non-snowy corner of the terrace wall with Keshkek and Muffin both resting beside me on the wall. They know a pretty day when they see one. We're all communing with nature together.

Craig went down the hill early to handle our problems. He told the *Comune of Pergine* that our road has been dug up by the pipe-line—and they had said we wouldn't be blocked. Craig drew them a picture and showed them that we are already blocked. The police chief and *geometra* (surveyor) came up to take a look. They witnessed Craig struggling to drive his car across the muddy field.

Then Craig went over to see Jeffrey to ask for his help on the pipe insulation issue. Jeffrey called his plumber who said that *tube* didn't need insulation. (The plumber is an idiot). He was finally convinced to come and bring insulation. Ermes said he would order some dry firewood for us. They were matter-of-fact—and not lovable. I think they're sick of us. Then Craig came home and stacked firewood. He did a good morning's work.

My fingers are too cold to write anymore and my butt is getting numb on this stone wall. So, I'll reluctantly part from this moment of feeling the joy of life—and loving a pretty day.

Surprise, surprise—Rolando, our plumber, came to our house with a friend this afternoon, and they have come up with yet another furnace solution.

Kitty just took a flying leap and landed in my lap where she is now purring passionately. She can be absolutely seductive at times.

Another bit of good fortune is that Kajsa and her daughter, Francesca—on winter break from Princeton University—arrived at the very moment the plumbers got here. They hiked over.

So, Francesca did a brilliant translation job. Would you believe it—the men put a temporary tank for the *gasolio* inside the furnace room and fed the *bruciatore* directly from there. That way the lines are not running along the ground from outside getting frozen. Our *gasolio*, which is too thick and of the worst quality, is still being used. We have the type *sud*, as compared to *mezzo* and *nord*. Southern Italy uses the type *sud* because it doesn't get cold there. Why Sguazzini, our *gasolio* man, sold us the type *sud* I'll never know. I think profit was his primary motivation.

Last year, we rented *Casanovalta* to a group of students from Cal Poly San Luis Obispo and their professor, Carlton Winslow, during the winter months. They had the same paraffin problem. Burbui claims he blew out the lines to the *gasolio* tank and fixed it. Why didn't he—or wouldn't he—blow out our lines this year? Why didn't he advise us on which *gasolio* to buy? Why didn't he tell Rolando all this sooner? We will still insulate the pipes to keep the *gasolio* from getting cold in the future. At present, the temporary solution is working.

February 20

It is Sunday at *Casanovalta* and the kitchen fire is blazing away, as are the radiators. The house is warm inside, while outside, the yucky sleet splashes down in 2°C weather. Craig has rallied from his cold and is outside stacking firewood. Kitty has climbed onto the woodpile and is delicately balanced at the tippy top. We're always waiting for the big crash. She is light on her feet—a cotton puff in the house—and a conscienceless killer outside. I will be making oatmeal cookies to give to our kind friends, the Zaccheos. On the surface we are serene.

Every time I cut my hair in an attempt to act like a grown-up, I regret it and yearn for my romantic tresses once more. I hate my hair. I look like Joan of Arc just before she was burned at the stake. The last thing in the world I need is to have ugly hair.

The Zaccheos were grateful for the cookies. Together, we munched a pile of them for tea—which flowed into an impromptu plate of spaghetti. They're good friends. Ugo lent me a typewriter, a manual portable Olivetti. I'm getting the typewriter cleaned and serviced.

February 21

Craig and I would have had a 9 a.m. appointment at the Pieve a Presciano bar with Ugo and Lazzari, the technician from the phone company, but Ugo telephoned in sick with a raging flu. We decided to postpone the discussion of the telephone poles until Ugo could make it. We need his creative suggestions and his translation. The phone man has a tremendous stutter—but is sweet, and seems sensitive. We hope to come to a good solution.

On psychologist Abraham Maslow's "priority of needs" list— from low to high, with the low requiring attention before the higher aspirations can be gratified—I cannot cross off one or two on the list of the lowest and most basic needs: #1 Proper shelter, and #2 Illness. But we're working on it and have the alternate heating system working now.

Craig and I went to the gasoline station and filled our 25 liter plastic water containers with diesel fuel (*gasolio*). These we walked up the hill— dragging them in the snow for a few paces, and then resting, and then dragging them some more, until we reached the house. I think all this walking up the hill is good exercise. We made the trip a second time. So, the house continues to be warm. The *bruciatore* motor was overtaxed from the thick oil and gave signs of breaking down. But we're hoping it will rally on this diet of warm, thin oil. Francesca, who runs the village bar, hooted at the yarn about three types of *gasolio—sud, mezzo,* and *nord*. She said, "There is only *gasolio*. You pay the same price for all of it." She said we should send the *carabinieri* (police) after Sguazzini, our *gasolio* man. I think we'd better send them after Burbui as well. Something seems inferior about the whole deal. We might as well lock up Pippo, the plumber, while we're at it.

On Sunday, Antonio will come to the house to start painting the interior plaster walls white. The end is in sight.

At long last, Roger Collins has sent us a postcard. This verges on
a miracle. I thought he and Mary didn't love us anymore. My best
friends from Los Angeles are not good correspondents. They visited us
at *Casanovalta* in 1980. My mom and dad have been our most faithful
correspondents. I wrote them a long letter last night. Correspondence is
our tip top priority.

February 27

Today, the tailpipe and muffler fell off the car when Craig was out
doing his errands. I think our bumpy road shook them loose. A nice
mechanic put them back. I had to go out in the evening in the rain
to buy house paint. We've caught eight mice in our mousetrap—ah,
home. The most darling thing has happened. Keshkek and Muffin have
become such good friends. They're so close and comfortable with each
other that they are now lying tail to tail, asleep on "Keshy's" pillow bed
for the very first time. They both looked up when they heard me move—
but they haven't budged because they're too cozy. Adorable. They've
found a way to be of mutual support to each other to ward off the icy
coldness of the house.

In this cold, wet, snowy, rainy, and windy weather, "Keshy's" best
effort on his "good night pee walk" is to walk to the edge of the front
porch and pee on it.

February 28

Yesterday, I was hugely creative and devoted the entire day to illustrating
and making drawings to scale, i.e. "designing" the downstairs dressing
room and bathroom. I enjoyed becoming involved in that familiar old
pastime. Today, Ugo Zaccheo, Craig, the SIP telephone technician,
and I walked down our country road looking at the land and planning
where to put our telephone poles so as not to bruise the beauty of the
landscape. Think of it—by March 20, we are likely to have a telephone.
Ugo will help us find a man to dig the ditch for putting the final part of
the line underground. We will have a telephone at last.

Spring

March 1

Spring came in "like a lion."

Today was a "*Casanovalta* day." I cleaned, fetched, carried, planned, and made decisions—in a joint effort with our *muratore*, Antonio. He has begun the giant project of finishing our house—at last. Now we will live with paint fumes in a house that is ripped apart. I was disgruntled to lose 100,000 lire out of my pocket after making the effort to go all the way to Arezzo to the paint store. I lost the money and had to leave half the materials I had intended to buy—and now must take the time to return there tomorrow. Truly, this was one of life's trying moments.

March 2

Work has begun today on our telephone installation. My heart is doing a happy dance.

March 4

Italian can openers don't work well on Italian dog food cans. I had to help Craig get a can open.

On another grim note, our trusted *muratore* did us dirt. He didn't properly clean the wall tile of cement stains before he applied varnish. He actually applied the varnish when the wall tiles were still wet, and thus did not show the grey. I questioned him about what he was doing, and he gave me a bunch of flimflam. He claimed that the tiles had sucked grey from the cement wall behind them. Craig said dryly, "That was not true." Now the work will have to be done all over again—by me. I am the best wall and tile cleaner around, plus house painter. I have proven myself by extensive labor over the years.

March 5

Another chapter unfolds in "As the Screw Turns," (the story of my life). The Electric Company of Italy had an uncontrolled burst of power that blew out a large transformer down by the *Montelucci* winery. They lost their utility power—and we not only lost our utility power but also the surge burned out the panel and wiring to our *autoclave*, (the pressure tank to bring water up into the house). One by one, we lost the *autoclave*, the motor to the radiators, the *bruciatore*, the well pump motor, the refrigerator—and the timer clock to the well started making erratic noises. I suggested to Craig that he turn off all the power at the breakers—fast.

This happened at dusk when I was slaving away on my hands and knees trying to scrub paint and cement off the living room floor. Prior to that, I had finished painting and tidying the living room. Antonio will return on Monday to find one room complete—after I oil the floor tomorrow.

As we were driving down the hill to meet Jeffrey and Ermes for dinner at *Le Cantine,* we saw an ENEL truck pull into *Fattoria Montelucci.* We followed the truck, and attempted to tell the men about our problem. They fixed the giant generator at the winery, and then followed us back up the hill to Casanovalta. With the power put back to normal, our machinery system started working again. But the *autoclave* was still, "*Guasto*" (busted). The repairmen suggested that Craig rewire it himself—"*Facile*" (easy), they said. Yeah, right. We will be without water in the house until the *autoclave* runs again.

I am surprisingly light-hearted, although my back is in muscle knots and spasms from overworking. No one but me seems to have the patience—or be willing—to do the hard work on the floors. Our muratore won't do it even if he's paid. I'll see if our new housekeeper will help me. She's another powerful woman.

March 6

I am exhausted. I have worked without pause the entire day—and find my basic temperament is very angry. The living room floor, which I had cleaned with *diluente* (solvent) and detergent the day before, still showed cement stains. So, I had to wash it all over again with pure muriatic acid and clear rinse water. My fingers are shriveled and raw. Fortunately, we had running water—because Craig discovered a tiny switch on the second circuit breaker in the transformer to the *autoclave.* He pushed it and everything started working again. So I had hot water with which to wash the floor.

I dusted, swept, vacuumed, and put everything in perfect order for Antonio to walk in and go to work tomorrow. A funny thing in Italy is that one sweeps the ceiling—as well as the walls and floors—especially in an old stone and tile house. There is a special long handled broom with a narrow flat brush for doing it. We do not expect Antonio to express one word of gratitude or praise. I find him insensitive to other people's feelings because he's so busy being sensitive to his own.

My little Muffin was terribly sick today. I fixed her a nest in my bed where she lay in a rumpled white ball. Then she shakily hobbled to the kitchen. Anticipating her need, I carried her out into the sun. She could only manage a high-pitched, faint mew. She lay in one place all day in the sun, then painfully dragged herself back inside when she got cold. She acted like even her hair hurt. She headed back to my bed and re-curled herself in the sheets and blanket nest. Tonight she had the strength to ask for some loving. Her nose was so dry it felt raspy. She knew I sympathized and felt deeply sorry for her. She probably ate a rotten rat.

March 7

When Antonio walked in the house and saw the finished living room, after our two days work, all he said was, "Pulito" (clean). This morning my neck, lower back, shoulders, arms, and buttocks ache. I have eight floors and two bathroom tile walls to go.

Upon reflection, I realize that Antonio is a product of his environment. He had an upbringing with a strict peasant father and deprivation. I know that I have an exaggerated need to be appreciated in order to compensate for my deeply felt sense of inadequacy. One may see the situation clearly, but one doesn't always know what to do about it.

Well praises be, I had a feeling my inner thoughts would rise up and bite me. Antonio asked me if I wanted to pause for lunch. I said, "No, I got a late start and am several hours behind on my schedule." And Antonio said, "It is because you have done so much work on Sunday. It is normal you should be tired." Ah, shucks—and Antonio had the flu with a bad throat and still came in to work. I expressed my sympathy and appreciation for the effort he was making on the ceiling. We are friends again.

March 8

I had a great deal of fun engaging in animated conversation and laughter with two girls who came over to our house last night, both are fiber, tapestry, and weaving artists—and are Kajsa's houseguests. One was from Australia and the other from Ireland. We were all speaking English—but "crikey" what a difference. We drank too much wine and stayed up too late. Craig was not amused. Today my marital relations have hit a new low—and I feel homesick for Los Angeles. In L.A. when I do my grocery shopping, I can stop for lunch at a delightful French restaurant. Here—nothing. I feel lonely. I lay in the sun with my dog and cat joining me—pretty scenery, but lonely. Craig and I are not getting along—and our house is torn apart by the mason.

March 9

Every morning lately, I have awakened feeling worried and muscle sore. Today I am praying for the *scavatura* to arrive. That piece of machinery is needed to dig the ditch for the phone line leading to our house. The phone men said they were ready to lay the line and would be leaving for Pieve a Presciano on Thursday. They are getting closer and closer.

The *scavatura* (clam digger) did not arrive. Gino Stopponi cannot come until Thursday. I had the feeling all along that the *scavatura* driver would be Gino. Gino is the "man with the machine" around here. He has dug all our ditches and laid the rock for our terrace walls. And when Raimondo said they would come on *"Lunedi, Martedì, or Mercoledì,"* I should have known enough about Italian psychology by now to know they meant *Mercoledì*, and more likely *Giovedì*. But fortunately, Raimondo and Vilmaro have come today and are digging the ditch between the house and the art studio by hand. They have explained the situation to the phone men. I think that everyone is satisfied. I was getting nervous about the whole thing. I am intensely eager to have the telephone sitting in the kitchen. The hassle of going to the public phone in Pergine has really worn thin on me.

Piano, piano (very softly) each day becomes warmer. I can wear fewer layers of clothing. I have eliminated the inner sweater layer and now put on a mere flannel shirt and a sweatshirt. I feel light and breezy in this attire. Last night, I didn't feel too cold as I sat writing at my typewriter. I feel inspired because there is warmth and prettiness to look forward to.

The Italians have various feast days with which to celebrate the coming of spring. First they have *Carnivale*, where on the last night everyone is dressed in costume. This is followed by Lent. But I haven't really seen anyone fasting. Yesterday, I saw women in the streets of Levane and Montevarchi carrying yellow-budded acacia branches. There was bustle and gaiety as it was the *"Giorno di la Donna"* (Lady's Day). I imagined lunch would be a proper feast. The villages of Levane and Montevarchi seem to have great fun on holidays.

Montevarchi, especially, seems to have a feeling of closeness unto itself—a real sense of community on festive occasions. Via Roma, the main street, has a promenade of young and old walking up and down and looking at each other every night, and especially on Friday night. They call it the "*passeggiata*." I can see how life passes more pleasantly with this type of group celebration and communal activity.

March 10

Every night recently my rest has been increasingly fitful from tense, sore muscles. The work level at the house yesterday was intense. Raimondo and Vilmaro were hand digging the telephone ditch. The telephone men were stringing up the line in the forest. Antonio was speedily painting away inside the house. Craig and I were feverishly clearing the way and cleaning up after. We're piling our possessions in one room to clear the way for the next. We have been covering the floor with giant sheets of plastic—because Craig accidentally bought a monster supply as a result of miscalculating meters for feet. We worked unflaggingly yesterday with a kindlier rapport.

Today, I will go with Kajsa to interview a maid to help me with housework. That is good of Kajsa—I really appreciate it. Last night, the Zaccheos gave an elegant dinner party for tapestry artist, Liz Nettleton-Seidel, in honor of her finishing the tapestries she was weaving. Kajsa admires her work, especially because she too is a weaver and has a large loom set up in her textile room at *La Fornace*. The Bavarian cream and champagne served were a touch of class.

Gino Stopponi did not come with the *scavatura* today. The telephone line is lying on the ground—and the telephone men have left. Gino says his clam digger is broken. So our telephone will have to wait until he comes with it—possibly tomorrow, but more probably on Monday. Patience is the primary virtue I have been practicing while living in Italy. I think Gino has another job and is lying.

Talking with the new maid at her home was interesting. Kajsa has a real feel for the local folksy style of conversation. In Tuscany, it is a common form of country civility to repeat a topic many, many times. Everyone knows the dialog and all the answers. They are in agreement. So everyone has the satisfaction of repeating something that was agreed upon, again and again. It expresses a sort of kindliness and camaraderie, and the desire to converse. Someone may ask you a question, (to which they know the answer), in order to give you the satisfaction of telling them again what everyone already knows. I've observed this conversational form often over the years. If you are in a hurry, it can be wearying. But I appreciate it for the companionable quality. In the old days, when there was no TV, this style of speaking could have probably spread out a conversation to last all evening.

Antonio is filling in a gap under a massive ceiling beam and secondary beams with *papier mâché*, a clever technique, and then gesso. He is essentially filling the gap with paper, flour, and water—and then plastering over it.

March 11

My day begins with the astonishing information that Stopponi has come with the *scavatura* (clam digger), and the very nice Raimondo, and Vilmaro have come as well. Raimondo is one of the most intelligent men around and has a quality of elegance about him. You would expect to see him sitting on the porch of a Southern mansion sipping a mint julep. Instead, he digs rock and cuts wood alongside Vilmaro. Both rough-cut country men must be over 60, and yet do backbreaking work. They are incredible. Raimondo speaks slowly so a *straniera* (foreigner) can understand him. Vilmaro is a lovable elf. This is such good news. I appreciate it even more after having waited for it. About Stopponi, I have my reservations. He is young and manly, and is part of the hard working, close knit village of Badia Agnano—as are Vilmaro and Raimondo.

Craig just told me the telephone men are here as well. It's our big day. I hear a horde of men yelling outside the front door. I better get going.

I'm as happy as I can be—sitting here in the midst of the clamor of working men. The great tractor has cleared land for our terraces, and I can imagine them finished. The telephone line is completely installed underground and the earth put back. The nettles and brambles are cleared from around our house. The caterpillar tractor roars and groans as it does its mighty earth moving work. Gino works its controls like a *ballerino* (ballet dancer). The older men are directing him as well. They are a perfectly coordinated ballet of manly power and prowess.

Craig and I were thrilled to discover on our land—buried under the overgrown weeds and nettles—an ancient solid stone animal drinking trough. It is made of a special stone called *pietra sirena*. You can see the markings of the stone mason's tool on the stone. We cherish it. Raimondo and Vilmaro have just placed the trough against our house, near the front entry to *Casanovalta*. It looks elegant there. This old house lends itself to beauty. All day, Craig has fulfilled his important role as the "big boss."

Even though there are no leaves on the trees and no spring flowers in sight, the season feels different. I walked around outside full of joy all day. My face was covered in smiles. Watching the men work was exciting. I applauded them. A good thing is that Raimondo and Vilmaro have decided to put us on the list of their preferred employers. We are honored. They are in the employ of the Zaccheos, Smart, Katz, Landau, Galli, and now us, the Ellwoods. We are pleased to join the club. Craig and I got the sense that they enjoyed working for us today. They also thought Keshkek was cute.

When I came home from the store, all the men were having a picnic together on the grassy knoll which looks out everywhere. "Keshy" ran tearing towards them when I let him out of the car. Antonio called out comically, *"Troppo tarde!"* (Too late). That really struck Craig and me as funny. But obviously Antonio was kidding because "Keshy" got his belly full. Keshkek too had a very happy day.

I drove the car to Siena this evening, for the first time, and took Kajsa and myself to a concert. Craig was too exhausted to attend. Kajsa and I saw duo-pianists playing Brahms. I especially liked the "Variation on a Theme by Haydn."

March 13

On a domestic note, out dog Keshkek imagined he was attending a picnic in the sky and licked the floor that Craig had acid washed yesterday and I had painted with *olio rosso*, a petroleum derivative product. Keshy was violently sick all over the house last night leaving mounds of foamy pink vomit everywhere—poor boy—and what a mess to clean up.

Our lunch at *Cennina*, a 9th–12th century castle, was a special treat. We dined outside in a small yard that was sheltered from the wind by remnants of the battlement walls. Our grassy patch caught the sun—which we savored on this first picnic of spring. A full budded peach tree arched over our heads. It too liked the warmth of the sun reflected by the castle wall.

Our menu, *ala* Osvaldo, was magnificent. For the antipasto we ate raw fresh onions and raw eggplant soaked in olive oil, lemon juice, and chopped garlic, with bread to sop it up. *Per pasta* (for the pasta), we savored a wide noodle in an amazing lemon peel, egg yolk, and cream sauce. Our entree was citrusy as well, duck l'orange—but rather more Tuscan because of the red wine and rosemary in the sauce. His potatoes and onions were darkly oven-browned. The *dolce* presented white cherries cresting a custard tart with an exquisitely flaky crust. Osvaldo cut a figure as he carried his great ceramic bowls of food from the scullery across the courtyard to our sunny niche. He was ceremoniously clad in a leather apron over his dark grey turtleneck sweater, and navy slacks.

Around coffee time, a group of curious tourists ambled through the courtyard and stared at us—while our charming lawn party group sipped coffee, soaked in the last rays of the day, and ruminated over how delicious our grand feast had been. Some of us gazed out beyond our immediate surroundings to the distant hills and the valley below. I could spot the route of the Algerian pipeline, and thus could follow its path to find *Casanovalta*. One of the guests rode home on his horse.

Refreshed by our sumptuous meal and splash of local color, Craig and I found the energy to move furniture for the *muratore* who will come tomorrow. Life grinds on at *Casanovalta*.

March 14

One of the nicest things about Osvaldo's party was that there were new faces, not just our normal incestuous group. Actually, it's a small group of locals who may gossip about each other—but who are, at the same time, concerned about one another. We keep tabs on each others' comings and goings. That being said, I find it comforting to know that there are other interesting people out there in the world.

One was a tall, blond American woman who is a graphic designer living in Perugia. She is helping the first costume museum in Italy get started. I found her humorous and intelligent. Her Italian escort seemed elegantly international, and also funny and kind. All *stranieri* (foreigners) at the party spoke excellent Italian. I enjoyed the gathering heartily.

That burst of spring yesterday has blown away today. It is windy, cold, grey, and threatening rain.

Our plumber has come and gone, and we are now back on the tank. He replaced, rather than "blew out," the lines to the tank. Craig had me come outside, as an allied force, to help him explain to the workers that he wanted extra insulation placed around the gas lines. Our good Raimondo and Vilmaro want to close the ditch without it. But they are conscientious enough to wait—since Craig wanted an extra tube placed around the whole deal. So Craig has frantically gone in search of ten meters of flexible tubing. He hopes to find it at the *Cooperativo* in Levane—as compared to tracking down Rolando, our long suffering plumber.

The men have cleaned the choking vines away from the row of cypress trees which shelters our house from the wind in the front. To our amazement, old crumbled terrace walls have been revealed and an ancient springhouse. It is called a *cisterna* (cistern). Vilmaro says he will repair the old walls. We have truly discovered a hidden treasure. The cistern was once the only water source for *Casanovalta*. They carried water to the house from the well.

Craig couldn't find the tubing. Vilmaro lost his patience. The workers have closed the ditch without it. My new maid and I acid washed floors all day long.

March 15

The "Ides of March," arriving with a ferocious wind, is our *quinto anniversario* (5th wedding anniversary). We called a halt to all workers and enjoyed a day of rest. We drove all the way to Castel Franco di Sopra to a restaurant we remembered enjoying, only to find it closed on Tuesdays. We handled this in good humor—even though we'd been counting on it and had dressed so nicely.

We asked a young policeman in the quaint piazza where to find a restaurant. He and an old lady described where to find one down the road. It was in a farmhouse set back from the road, which made us afraid that it was going to be hideously *casalinga* (homestyle cooking). To our great delight, and through the lucky hand of fate, it turned out to specialize in seafood. They had another restaurant at the beach. Our hot shellfish antipasto brought back happy memories of our summer vacations by the sea. A spring daffodil brightened the table. We had a good anniversary lunch after all.

March 17

The world moves at a sleepy pace today and the weather is grey, rainy, and tinged with cold. Remo and Giuseppina, our local butcher and his dominating wife who runs the show, served customers at a lethargic pace. Giuseppina is twice the size of Remo and sports a small dark mustache on her upper lip. She barks orders at Remo in her deep voice and drones laconically to each customer, "*Poi, poi?*" (next, what then?)—as she serves them methodically, one by one, item by item. Remo drags around chopping meat, and seems to be gone for long periods of time in the meat locker. His hands are red and raw from the cold, and incessant chopping of bloody meat. In happy contrast, I ran into my dark-bearded French-Swiss friend, Bernard, who was selling pecorino cheese that he and his wife are now making at their farm near Siena. Josepina has been trying out some rounds to see how they sell. Bernard gave me one as a gift. It was soft sheep cheese, moist and delicate—just the way I like it.

At the bread store, the baker's wife asked me if I have children—as she does every time I go in there. I said that I don't. She replied comfortingly that I was young yet—as she always does. I feel like my privacy is being invaded.

On the road returning home, I saw an old woman who has a face like the "mask of tragedy." She is a peasant woman who truly looks like she witnessed the war. World War II raged through this part of Tuscany. In fact on the hill where *Casanovalta* sits, the British fought against the Italians. Bullet shells can still be found dug into the earth. In Pergine, hand written words left on a wall in the village state for all time, "Shemtov slept here."

At 1p.m. in the country, there is absolutely nothing else to do but go home and eat lunch. The men like to have their coffee at the local bar in town—but I have nowhere to go but home. I miss Michel Richard—my favorite French cafe in Los Angeles, so very much.

Antonio, our *muratore*, and I have an unusual rapport. We are totally different. He is a devout materialist and calls me a "spiritualist." We have a running battle, as he challenges everything I say about psychology and metaphysics in an emphatic and aggressively independent way. He thinks what he thinks—case closed. And he thinks a great deal as he is highly intelligent. Antonio had only two years of formal education. His motto is, "Work!"—which he does every day of the week including Sunday, especially Sunday. He is building his own house, and is a building crew of one man. Today I commented that I couldn't get my motor going. He said that his was going slowly too. I wondered out loud if our "personal tempos" might be slower today—or if they were always the same? He told me I shouldn't think about things like that so much. He said, "If one were to hit his finger with a hammer but not think about it, it wouldn't hurt as much." I thought he had a point there—but I wondered if he knew he was being rather metaphysical. I don't have a good enough command of Italian to have equal opportunity to express myself—or defend myself.

Antonio and Craig are teaching each other Italian and English. I think they're cute together. Tomorrow, Antonio will devote the day to cooking fish at our house.

I'm sleeping downstairs now in the ex-stable, which is surprisingly cozy. I like it. The peasants who lived at *Casanovalta* once raised flocks of sheep. Livestock was stabled under the house, and the stalls remain where they once were kept. The animal body warmth probably contributed to the heating the house. Our upstairs bathroom used to be the cheese room.

March 18

I lie here with a heavy stomach and aching feet. Today Antonio cooked. I never witnessed anyone cook like that in my life. He was the "big boss" today commanding me to, "Wash this skillet and wash that,"— and asking me, "Where is such and such, and that other thing?" Craig and I really hustled to keep up with Antonio's pace. The two of them went to Montevarchi early this morning to buy the fish, 100,000. lire worth. Craig set up the dining room beautifully with numerous candles and yellow wild-flowers called *maggio*. They emit a subtle sweet aroma. Traditionally, those long stemmed brilliantly yellow flowers bloom in May. They grow prolifically and adorn the countryside.

After tidying up the house, we hopped to attention to assist Antonio. At one point, we pulled at least 100 *lumache* (tiny sea snails) out of their shells to go into various dishes. We gaped in amazement and applauded as we witnessed the grand preparations. Antonio was a man who knew his job.

He steamed clams and mussels to open them and saved the cooking broth for his paella. He steamed the "snails of the sea" and we ate some for lunch in *olio, aglio, e peperoncino* (olive oil, garlic, and hot red flaked pepper). Liz and Mary, the Irish and Australian tapestry artists, dropped by for awhile to assist in the kitchen. They "hopped to" properly, but muttered under their breaths, "Antonio is rather bossy."

For the entire day, Antonio teased me unmercifully about only feeding Craig *Sofficini* (a freezer-style crepe stuffed with cheese, touted on Italian television). At dinner Antonio served me, as my *primo piatto* (first course), a frozen package of Sofficini and a can opener. Humph. I felt insulted. Antonio was trying to teach me to do my duty and cook nicely for Craig, like a good Italian housewife.

Today Antonio cooked an excess of food in the grand Italian tradition—ten courses in all.

Count them:

For antipasto, we ate raw anchovies "cooked" in lemon juice, and steamed mussels bathed in olive oil, lemon juice, and chopped garlic.

For the pasta, we ate a giant bowl of paella made with beef broth, sautéed beef and pork, sausage, mussels, squid, shrimp, and heavily seasoned with saffron.

Then the fish dish entrees started:

- red mullet fried in a piquant sauce.
- octopus in a laurel leaf, pine nut and raisin sauce, with toast prepared in the fireplace.
- a *crostata* (pan pizza with a top crust) filled with mussels, oregano, and tomato.
- sole dipped in orange juice and coated with bread crumbs, which was then fried along with little shrimps, then topped with pine nuts, raisins, and laurel sauce.
- squid stuffed with breadcrumbs, that were mixed with finely minced parsley, garlic, and olive oil.
- trout, stuffed with the same thing, grilled over the fireplace.

- red peppers roasted in the fireplace, then skinned and pulled into strips.

We washed it all down with liters of *Tocai*, our local white wine. As Mary, one of our dinner guests remarked, "We have had an elegant sufficiency." I've taken an Alka Seltzer and will face the kitchen tomorrow.

March 19

A day of sun—hung—dishes done.

March 20

Another day of sun has passed and more Alka Seltzer ingested. Craig and I had lunch at the home of our kind postmaster. He is a dear man with a friendly family —although his son and daughter suffer from the normal problems of adolescence and young adulthood. They're our good friends—and we're grateful for them.

After lunch, I lay in the sun to catch the last rays. The animals did something endearing which I never saw them do before. Keshkek lay down beside me on the mat with his head plunked on my breast. Muffin chose to sit dead center on my chest. "Keshy" gave her a lick in the face and she licked him back. After gently licking his head six times, she started to give him a proper grooming. He jumped when her raspy tongue hit his nose, but lay there with a dreamy look in his eyes as she licked his forehead, neck, and down his flopped out ear—(much bigger than a kitty's ear). I felt love for them swell in my heart.

After painting linseed oil on half a floor and scrubbing the fireplace mantle, I'm off to bed. I feel yucky and hope I never have to eat again.

Tomorrow, Antonio will paint the kitchen. Craig and I moved everything out. We will love having fresh white walls—and eventually the serenity of our home restored.

March 21

I'm still trying to awaken and feel deeply tired with sore muscles. During the night, I clicked off my electric blanket and threw off a cover because the weather felt so hot.

This day felt painful for me. Antonio was in a surly mood—(after so much bonhomie). Craig went to bed with a backache and stayed there all day.

Of all the messes, the kitchen being ripped apart is the most disturbing. And to top it off—at noon, when I was about to go down to Pergine to make some phone calls, Antonio asked me, "Where are you going?" I told him,"To Pergine." Then, at that late moment he told me, (in an insolent sort of way), that he didn't have the white paint to paint the kitchen. I offered to go to Ponticino to get it. But it turned out, (as anyone should have known), that stores are closed on Monday mornings in Ponticino.

The priest in Ponticino, dressed in his cassock, was walking down main street benevolently blessing the houses and charming the women. Later, he was leading a funeral procession on foot with a small army of altar boys accompanying him and the townsfolk following behind. The Pergine priest has also been busy blessing the houses for Easter. I felt cheered by the happy springtime bustle in my town, Pergine.

Back up the hill, the tension remained. I went back down at 3 p.m., when I was told the paint store would open, then rushed back home with the big container of paint exclaiming triumphantly, *"Ecco fatto – altri trenta chili di vernice!"* (Here you are, done —another 30 kilograms of paint). Antonio replied cooly, (something that might translate into), "As you wish"—as if it were *my* idea to get the paint, as if he hadn't told me the little bit of white paint remaining wasn't sufficient to finish painting the kitchen, and as though it wasn't his responsibility to know he was running out of paint and tell me sooner—like the Thursday before. I swallowed hard on that one and went into a slow burn. I felt sad, bad, and mad. Language felt like a huge barrier. I sat on the kitchen step and debated whether or not to take issue—whether the battle was worth it. I got sadder and madder. So I went to the car and lugged the heavy can of paint out of the trunk and into the kitchen. I managed to find the courage and energy to express myself.

I said, "Antonio, when I have made two trips down the hill to buy paint, why can't you say, 'Thank you?'" He replied, "Why should I say 'thank you'?"

I said, "Because, I have done you a favor."

He said mockingly, "Oh, is it *my* paint? And what you want me to say is *'thank you'*? All right then, 'thank you'."

I muttered an anguished, "Thank you," and turned on my heels to rush outside—because I found to my embarrassment that I was about to burst into tears. He called something joking after me which I didn't catch. I stood behind the house with hurt tears oozing out of my eyes. Muffin and Keshkek both hurried over to comfort me. My life felt lonely and bleak. However, when I went back inside to work some more on the floors, I sensed a kinder tone.

Later that evening, Craig and I went shopping in Arezzo. Specifically, I was in search of a metronome to test "personal tempo," a semi-scientific interest and theory of mine that I am developing. I found the music store and chose a pocket-size metronome. I tested Craig and myself to determine how best to conduct a general test of others. I thought maybe someone could beat out a tempo on a tabletop, which represented how they were feeling inside—and then I could find that same tempo on the metronome. I think it is best for someone not to hear another person beating their tempo, because that could interfere with their own natural rhythm. Before I went to bed my beat was 168. Craig's was 184. I wonder if my beat was slower from when I did it in the car? I could have been influenced by Craig. I may end up getting an electric metronome for more accuracy. For some reason, I am fascinated by the sense of everyone having their own "personal tempo." And I ponder, "Do tempos interact? How do we affect others with our tempo?"

Italy is boring at night in the country.

March 22

Kitty found me. She loves me she does. Her little face was pressing through the bars of the cross-hatched wood of the ground floor stall window. She mewed insistently until I got up to open the window. She has finally figured out where I moved to because she misses our ritual of "good morning loving." Now she is well and truly pummeling my stomach with her paws and purring in my face. I have to laugh out loud.

My stomach feels like I'm creating an ulcer. So I'll take my poor tummy upstairs for something gentle and milky to eat. I'll also ease up on the negative thoughts. Kitty is blissfully grooming herself in expectation of settling down beside me for a nap while I read in bed. Unfortunately, that is only a remembered ritual because now I must do my housecleaning labor. (I'll work on having a better attitude. Love is the way).

March 23

Wrong—I bottomed out and am staggering under the blow of "Tuscan gossip." But I have managed to come up a winner in the end.

On my way to Siena yesterday, I stopped by Kajsa Zaccheo's estate, *La Fornace,* to tell her I was going to buy concert tickets. Her husband, Ugo, was due home from Mexico at any minute. Therefore she seemed to be stressed, rigid, and insensitive to incoming messages and nuances—and unknowingly insensitive to me as she told me her maid's story. Kajsa's vocal intonation sounded almost exactly like her maid. Hearing the story made me feel like I'd been kicked in the stomach by a horse. But I had enough presence to protest to Kajsa that she knew her maid was a gossip and told distorted tales.

Apparently, Kajsa's maid came to Kajsa with the information that my new maid, Paola, had told her—to tell Kajsa—to tell me—that Paola was insulted because I had "sent her away" on Friday, the day of our fish fry, and that "she wouldn't stand to be treated like that and wasn't sure if she wanted to work for me anymore. There were too many things to be done, ironing for instance, and the road was just too bad—and she didn't think she wanted to make the trip."

I felt sick at heart. It seemed so difficult to understand people in a foreign land. We had made the arrangement with Paola that she was to come on Thursday, if she didn't get called to the old folk's home to work. She did not come to my home on Thursday—so it was clear that she'd been called to work elsewhere. To my surprise, she showed up on Friday in the midst of the party clamor. My sense was that she had come to show her good will. The confusion was too great and I couldn't think of another thing—so I said I didn't think she needed to work that day. We parted amicably with an arranged date for her return.

So this twisted "alternate information" really did a job on my "ulcer." My stomach burned and I felt faint as I walked in the streets of Siena. In Siena the world was ablaze with color—happy, lively, exciting. School children of all ages were everywhere. I bought the theatre tickets and went by the *Scuola di Lingua per Stranieri* (Language School for Foreigners) for information. I wished I could live in Siena and attend school. On the way home, I felt farther and farther away from civilization.

When I told Craig the pathetic story about the mis-communication with the maid, I felt desperately sad. This was the day she was to come. When the agreed upon hour came and went, I was afraid that Kajsa's maid's story was true. Craig and I couldn't understand how anyone could be that touchy. I felt especially hurt because I thought that Paola and I had felt a fondness for each other.

The thought of acid washing all the floors in the house by myself was a burden I couldn't bear. So I told Craig that I was going to her house on bended knee to plead for her forgiveness and beg her to come back. But just as I was going out the kitchen door, there stood Paola. I fell on her in an embrace. She hugged me back. She was calm, smiling, relaxed, and slightly surprised at my excessive emotion. I told her how happy I was to see her and how sorry I was about Friday. Paola assured me that everything was perfectly all right, and she had only passed by to see if she was needed. So delirious with joy, I got her the equipment to acid wash yet another floor. And she, with a very good attitude, set to work.

I felt so shaken up by the experience my stomach became an acid knot. I could barely eat a cream soup. At bedtime, Craig and I were both exhausted. We took hot baths and crashed into bed.

To his own personal satisfaction, Antonio finished painting the kitchen yesterday. He sniggered at my scene with Paola and commented that I was like a baby. (He didn't know the whole story).

Today I have stayed in bed all morning. It's time to get up. Antonio is outside cutting stone for the terraces. I'm certain he thinks Craig and I are soft. We are—but I prefer it that way. It's a more comfortable way to live. I know I'm doing the very best I can do. When I push myself to do more, I collapse. I can't live up to the Zaccheo's standards either. I can't even live up to my own. So I'll just keep on making the best of it.

By the position and the nature of the pain, it has suddenly dawned on me what is my physical problem. It's my hernia. The hernia, once repaired by my chiropractor in Florence, Dr. Kinnard, pushes a piece of my stomach through my diaphragm into my esophagus causing an acid feeling. I feel relieved to have figured out the source of my distress. I can give up my hypochondriacal imaginings. But what to do about it?

To my embarrassment, Ugo Zaccheo walked into our house through the unlocked front door, just as I was walking into the kitchen wearing my bathrobe. I explained defensively, "I'm sick." He was looking for a ride down the hill, but Craig had already gone with the car. Aside from the white walls in the kitchen, the house looked like a bloody mess— damn it. I'm always getting caught by Ugo. I wonder if he'll ever find me coiffed, with an immaculate house, doing something constructive. I must brazen it out.

Today ended up being a big construction day on the terraces. But it began with Antonio doing a noisy number on our heads about, "How can I do the work without materials?" Antonio ranted at me about how he needed a truckload of rock, etc. etc. (as I was hanging out the wash), as well as chiding me for sleeping late, blah, blah. I told him I would find Craig, and we would bring a pad of paper and a pencil so we could make a list of everything that was needed. I reasoned with him, "I thought that list making was what we were supposed to be doing today."

Craig ended up going down the hill with Antonio to round up all the materials. He decided to give Antonio a piece of his mind. *"Non blah blah blah forte a me! Non mi piace!"* (Don't blabber loudly at me. I don't like it). This was especially true because it was Antonio's responsibility to tell us in advance about all the materials he would need. He had known for four weeks that we were going to be finishing the terraces.

Fortunately, Gino Stopponi and Luciano instantly came up our hill with a truckload of gravel and forty bags of cement. All this went on while I was putting the kitchen back in order; washing, sweeping, dusting. And then I brushed linseed oil on my bedroom floor while clutching my burning hernia and intermittently drinking yogurt, or cream of chicken soup.

Two things in Antonio's favor; he graciously said to me, *"Buona sera"* (good evening) as he left, (which I took as a peace offering), and he told Craig, *"Sono d'accordo"* (I agree) re: Craig's complaint.

I told Craig, "I think we should compliment each other for the fine job and unbelievably hard work we're doing, because it obviously isn't coming from any other source." (I do not feel understood). I consider myself fine-boned with a sensitive nervous system—as compared to being a big-boned plow horse. I am a lady not a *contadina* (country woman). And one thing is for sure—I am sick of workers at my house. I want some privacy and peace. As I kissed Craig goodnight he said, "I give you pity and praise." I laughed and said, "That would make a good title for a chapter in my journal."

During this season in farm country, the olive trees and grape vines are being pruned, and the ground is being plowed for sowing seeds. Spring is in the air.

March 24

I spent a rainy day in Florence attempting to renew my passport—not having any success but remaining cheerful. I must warm my wet feet in bed now. I got rained on.

March 25

It is 1:30 a.m. and I am in bed. I've just returned from hearing The London Early Music Group, directed by James Tyler, in Siena. I especially liked the Parisian 15th century dance music. The applause at the *Academia Chigiana* is always very warm. We responded enthusiastically to Tyler's virtuosity on a mini-mandolin. The old instruments were amazing. The ancient violin had an oddly short bow which didn't allow for much vibrato in the tone. The violin was dark with age.

For our trip to Siena, even though it was raining, I dressed up in high heels to feel like a girl again—after brushing linseed oil on two floors. Craig sympathizes that no Italian men ever seem to be around when I am working. I have hurt feelings because Vilmaro, who I like and who I thought liked me, told Ermes that I am hopeless. He claimed that I sat around and watched him—the day he worked at our house— instead of working. (I had been applauding Raimondo and Vilmaro on their work—plus directing two other workers, and the telephone linemen). Besides, I was celebrating the first warm day of spring. The second time they came to work at *Casanovalta*, I had my hair in a bandana and was slaving away on sweeping ceilings and oiling floors— but they didn't tell Ermes about that.

I shouldn't let something like this get to me—but I find gossip, by its nature, vicious and untrue. But people also believe it. What is it about villages and the country that creates small minds and gossip? I'm tired of living in the provincial atmosphere of the country. I'm tired of "Tuscan gossip." I yearn for a broader, more worldly, open viewpoint.

I miss being in tune spiritually. I miss feeling understood. I miss my friends Sheila, Mary, and Faye. I miss being able to walk out the front door and not step ankle deep into mud.

I have planned a trip to *Milano* for Craig and me. It is my intention to meet Baba Bedi, the beloved guru of Carla Staderini, a Roman psychotherapist I know. Baba Bedi taught her Expressive Arts Therapy techniques. I'm interested in that topic. Maybe this exploration will help me get a grip on my well-being. I've been feeling angry and weepy.

March 26

I woke up yearning for my friends, the ones who love me and with whom I feel deep rapport, the ones I love. *Casanovalta* feels so far from everything. (We didn't know that when we bought it and spent all these years reconstructing it). The people of Pieve a Presciano are amazed that someone is again living at *Casanovalta*. They like to see the light burning on the hill to show that it is inhabited. Ugo said the people living at *Casanovalta* used to go down to Pieve once a month. I said, "So do we." Craig laughed.

I used to have a fantasy that I would have a baby here and watch it play in the meadow—sunlight in its hair. But that seems so long ago and far away.

This day has turned out so much better than I could ever believe. I went upstairs, from my sheep-stall room, into the kitchen—where Craig was finishing his French toast with *preiselbeere* (lingonberries) and said, "I have some thunder-striking news." (That got his attention). I continued, "Maybe because it's spring, but—I want to have a baby." He answered calmly, "Well, all right, let's have one." I started to look at the calendar to figure out the days of my cycle—but Craig took me in his arms—and I misted over in tears.

I have felt cheerful all day and worked very hard at Paola's side. She came in the afternoon, all smiles.

When Craig and I went down the hill to Pergine for mail and to make local phone calls, we had a jolly moment at the town bar where we ran into John Cheyne, who was wearing in his riding gear. His Pergine riding school and stables are up and running. It was good to kid around in English with our old buddy. He cut a handsome figure in his formal horseman's attire.

At home, we had tacos for lunch for the third day in a row. A friend of Craig's mailed us four cans of *tortillas* from Texas, "Ashley's of El Paso"—yahoo. What a blessed relief—they are tasty little morsels, those critters. And for dinner, I made Indonesian "Nasi Goreng," complete with fried bananas—nothing Italian all day.

Paola acid washed the dining room and plain washed the kitchen floors. I applied linseed oil to the living room floor for the last time—next comes bee's wax. Craig and I sat in the kitchen and thought the house looked brilliantly beautiful. We sat and stared at it.

March 27

My day began with, "Anita, we've got a problem!"

So from 10a.m. to 7p.m., I have been swabbing the living room floor with gasoline. Craig scrubbed in my bedroom. We scoured and scoured, tile by tile, to cut the rubbery glaze crusting on the surface of many tiles. Disastrously, I had used an old can of linseed oil that was too dense—which had caused the oil to gum up on the surface before the tile could absorb it. I had, in essence, destroyed the beauty of the bathroom, my bedroom, and the living room floors.

The living room, which had the original antique floor, was my pride and joy. I had already applied two coats of red oil, as well as one coat of linseed oil on it. For good measure, to do the job really right, I put on one last coat—of the tainted oil. So all day I have desperately scrubbed, with everything in me, to save the tile. My knees are two raw red blotches. The house reeks of gasoline. But, by God, we broke up the glaze. The floors still have a semi-shiny patchiness—but the permanently sticky crust is gone. I gave the living room floor a second "painting" with gasoline. I find a morbid fascination in observing how some of the tiles are discoloring into lighter terra-cotta tones. The next step will be to put bee's wax on the living room floor. I hope against hope that it will even up the color and sheen.

Through all of this I have been heroic, energetic, and cheerful. I forced Craig to smile. He was the one who realized the terrible problem we were facing—and the solution of using gasoline. But he kept grieving over all the hard work I'd done—and the more hard work to come. I insisted that he cheer up. He rose to the occasion—bad back and all. We saved the day.

Tonight, we packed for *Milano*. My back is in knots. Ah, bed. I'm looking forward to our trip.

March 28

The muscles of my right hand are fatigued. I shall raise up this muscle sore body and go to *Milano*. The weather has had a cold snap—an Easter tradition, I suppose. The Pratomagno mountains have a fresh cap of snow. My knees are red, sore, and raw.

March 30

Blissed out in *Milano*. I love *Milano*. This town is so civilized and bustling; urbane and friendly; sophisticated and natural; elegant and casual. We are rapturous being here—simply enraptured with *Milano*.

Our self-contained loft-flat is on the *Corso Porta Vigentina*—with a tram stop outside the door. Signor Vittoriano Vigano, *architetto*, (architect) has his modern office in the 18th century building next door. We are his guests in the red, black and grey modern flat he designed for his daughters' private use. Our inner courtyard looks at an elegant carriage-house apartment, and a sky-lighted sculptor's pad. We are ten minutes by tram from the *Duomo* (cathedral)—how luxurious to be living in a civilized place.

Craig and I like bringing back sandwiches from the bar across the street and getting an extra cappuccino in the morning. A cheese shop and a fruit shop are next door. A few blocks away, on Corso Porta Romana, is our favorite *Antico Forno* (antique oven) bread shop. We will buy scrumptious *"panfornaio"* (baker) cookies for Osvaldo, and Easter at *Castelo Ceninna*. The shop people are respectful and kind in *Milano*. The citizens are polite on the tram.

We've had personal success. Craig was welcomed warmly by his gallery owner, Bruno Lorenzelli. We had lunch with him and his sweet wife today at *da Bice,* an excellent insider's restaurant near the *Via Spiga*. The lunch crowd was jumping. We like being shown the right places by Lorenzelli. He has humor and style, and knows how to live well. He called a good gallery in Zurich for Craig. The idea is that Craig will have an exhibit in Zurich, and then come back to the Lorenzelli Gallery in *Milano*. Craig feels good about this.

I feel fantastic to have been given a great haircut by *Enrico's*. I walked in as "St. Joan" and came out like a "lion." I look like I have more hair after a haircut than before. I have been re-born. I can hold my head up high again. Thank God. All winter I have suffered looking like a jerk. Now I can feel better about myself.

Pasqua (Easter) seems to be a really happy time in Italy. Shops all over Milan have egg decorations in the windows. Everyone is wishing the next person, *"Auguri!"* (congratulations). The dove is another baked and molded design. The weather has become milder and forsythia are in bloom. The garden of the *Poldi Pezzoli* museum is a panoply of spring with bursting sprigs *of forsythia. We walked from the Piazza Duomo,* through the *Galleria,* to the *Piazza Scala;* up *Via Mazzoni,* and then right onto *Monte Napoleone,* with its ultra-chic designer shops. Tomorrow we will go into a sumptuous delicatessen, that has numerous *pâtes* in gelatin in the window, to see if they carry lingonberries. Craig and I have a special fondness for lingonberries. Their Easter display is the *crème de la crème.* I would haunt that shop if I lived in *Milano.* From there we walked to *Via St. Andrea* to meet Lorenzelli at the *Galleria.*

Tomorrow evening, we will drive to an outlying district to meet Baba Bedi—or "Baba Baby," as Craig has nicknamed him.

March 31

Baba Bedi was my first Indian guru. I have had spiritual teachers before—but never a real guru.

My sense of unreality increased as we navigated through intricate Milan traffic to discover an apartment district in an outlying zone. Craig parked the car and said he would wait for me there. A little girl directed me along a serpentine path to *scala* 4 (stairway #4). I felt greatly relieved to read *Baba Bedi* on the buzzer. A pretty young woman with cascading brown hair, who introduced herself as Antonia, let me into the apartment. I immediately saw Baba Bedi sitting in a hospital-type bed with a food tray before him holding the remains of his dinner and some medicine bottles. He seemed to be very old and in pain. At first, he appeared to be toothless and shrunken down. He leaned sideways on a pile of pillows with one bare foot sticking out and resting on a stool. I felt a little bit shy because I had never spoken to an Indian guru before, and also felt shocked and sad to see that he was sick. I was reminded of my beloved metaphysics teachers, Helen and Nancy Featherstone. I wondered what a guru, who was an energy healer, was doing being sick? But it seems that great teachers often do get sick. I did not mention his sickness, out of politeness and inhibition. I now think I should have been more honest and asked him about his health.

Nevertheless, I found him to be very warm and friendly. He smoked a Gitane cigarette—then we began talking. He seemed to gain strength as he talked to me. I had to listen carefully because of his Indian accent, his minimal teeth, and the noise a giant St. Bernard dog was making chewing on his squeaky toy. The monster dog had ambled out to greet me, presented his great head to be stroked, then settled down beside me with his squeeze ball. The Italian girl, Antonia, laughed at his sociability. She was present as secretary and coordinator. I realized later, because I saw a conference brochure with her name written on it as Antonia Bedi, that she must be his wife.

The "Baba" told me about the five steps he taught for developing psychic sensitivity and spiritual healing. We discussed how I might be able to study with him, and what it was I wanted to know. I explained my connection with Carla Staderini, the Expressive Arts Therapist, and my desire to know if I was on the right path.

He said, "I see much energy around your hands—which could explain why you are feeling compelled to go into the healing arts."

He continued, "You have done well with your life because you have listened to your inner voice—and have gone with your inner urges."

I said, "Yes, I have always followed my feeling."

He asked me, "Do you know why you have the urge to do one thing as compared to another?"

I replied, "I don't really know."

He stated, "*It is because you have the potential to do it.*"

Baba Bedi signaled the end of the interview—and we parted as new friends.

His final words were, "*There are no obstacles—they have a way of vanishing.*"

I pondered that thought.

April 1

We are back home again in the stillness of the country—oh, how I miss the roar of the tram.

My dog and I walked the hilltop fields and found spring violets on the moist forest floor. I gazed through our new telephone poles on the ridge, across the valley, and out to the misty hills beyond.

I can't find my diamond wedding ring where I remembered putting it on the kitchen countertop. I put it there before I was distracted by the linseed oil and gasoline disaster. Then we left our house in the hands of the house-sitter who likes to entertain in our absence. I feel worried and bad. This has been my homecoming.

April 2

I woke up today with that *Casanovalta* lonely feeling. I dreamt that I found my ring under a piece of paper on the table in the music room. Feeling happy in spite of myself, I have made peanut butter cookies for Easter. Outside there is patchy sun and rain—brrrr, cold.

It is Easter Eve. The cookies I made taste yummy with milk. I wish I had my ring.

EASTER

April 3

Easter felt sad and not holy enough—the crowd was too drunk and rowdy at *Cennina*.

We arrived too late. Osvaldo's brother, Italo, is dying. This caught Craig and me by surprise.

I felt distressed to see Italo ill. Osvaldo danced to keep the crowd lively. His whole family danced; his old mother, sister, and baby niece. I cried inside. Were they crying inside as well?

Back at *Casanovalta*, we wrote—I in my journal, and Craig a long letter home. We both were feeling too vulnerable.

April 4

The Easter event yesterday had the quality of a bad dream. As Craig and I were arriving at *Castello di Cennina*, we saw two women we knew leaving. They were already traversing the steep path down the hill. They called out, "You're too late. Everything's been eaten. Perhaps you could gnaw on a bone."

When we entered the inner courtyard we saw great white ceramic eggs, the elegant white pottery made at Ceninna, on long empty tables. We saw an American woman we knew and liked, and waved to her. The man she was talking to turned around. It was Osvaldo's brother, Italo—

with his face blown up twice its former size. His arm was in a sling. Hiding my shock, I kissed him on both cheeks.

I went upstairs into the house to find Osvaldo, and give him the cookies we brought from *Milano*. He was dancing a Tango in the middle of a crowded room full of drunk people. He grabbed me and made me dance. I tried to dance. He took the box of cookies I offered him and threw it across the room to a fat Italian man who sat sprawling in the middle of a couch, his bulbous belly rising up and his pudgy legs splayed out.

As Osvaldo and I were dancing, the man asked me, "Are you *Tedesca?*" (German) I answered, "No, American." He said sardonically, "Oh, Canadian?" I said, "No, Californian."

He made a joke about me in Italian that I couldn't understand—and everyone laughed at me.

With as much dignity as I could muster, I got the box of cookies back from the fat man. I opened the paper and offered them to Osvaldo's French mother, his sister, and to him. He suggested that I offer the cookies to a man whose lap he had sat me in as we were dancing. Then Osvaldo snatched the cookies and offered them to the fat man again—saying he would eat them all. I took back the box of cookies and set them on a table. I ate three, because I was starving, then escaped.

Later, Craig and I went up to the living room together. We watched Osvaldo dance on the tiny patch of floor. Osvaldo's baby niece danced, floodlit by rays of dust-filled light from the ancient castle window. Osvaldo threw one of her big chocolate Easter eggs around the room— and finally to the fat man. He missed catching it, and it fell to the floor and shattered. Craig and I said we had to leave and find something to eat. The pretty wife of the fat man suggested we go down to the kitchen and snack on left-overs. (How had we missed knowing the correct time to arrive for the party?) The fat man asked Craig, "Do you want to trade women?" Craig responded coldly, "You should ask the women first."

We went down to the scullery and found some bread and cheese, beans, and rice pudding. There was a ceramic bowl full of green artichokes and eggs—a pretty display. We snacked on crusts and decided to leave. Osvaldo pleaded with us to "Stay." But we bid him *"Buona Pasqua"* (Happy Easter) and fled.

We passed boys in a bicycle race on the road. Driving through Pieve a Presciano, we stopped by Ermes' house for a visit because we felt lonely. He gave us coffee and toast. Then we went home to write and write.

This morning, the day after Easter, I opened my bedroom window to see flakes of snowfall outside—driving snow. We laughed. From the smoldering ashes rises the Phoenix.

Craig and I had a great day playing soft rock music on the radio and bouncily putting the house back into order. We reassembled the antique curved-iron twin beds in my room, moved old chests, and washed and oiled floors in harmony. My haven is again in order and peaceful. The floor in my bedroom seems too dark—but it will do. The furniture hides most of it.

Ugo Zaccheo and friends dropped by unannounced, as is typical. He found us working—yay. He invited us over for a post-Easter dinner— which felt just right. I was delighted and felt a strong affection for the Zaccheos.

The evening was full of laughs. One set of friends was visiting from *Milano*—the wife was Chinese and in the fashion business. She bought in Italy for her shops in Hong Kong. I liked her very much and felt a strong rapport. Her husband was a humorous, sophisticated, and charming Italian. She was leaving for Paris the next day. A young Australian chap, with a great grin, was the other guest.

April 5

I reached into the laundry basket to get my dirty blue jeans to put in the wash—and peeping out of a pocket was the glint of gold. I tremulously hauled my jeans out of the dark depths to reveal the glitter of a diamond. I found my wedding ring. It was looped onto my favorite gold bracelet. Both had been tucked into the pocket of my blue jeans. I clutched them to my breast and said a prayer of gratitude, "Oh, thank God!" I was super industrious today, while cleaning the house and doing errands. I felt ecstatic with relief.

Yesterday, Craig and I saw our first up close, in broad daylight, wild boars. They really had razor backs with an arch of long bristly hair rising on their backs. I never saw this phenomenon on a stuffed one. The faces and snouts were amazingly long and dished, a long straight line distending from their little-bitty eyes up by their pointy ears. We were driving down the Montelucci road and saw this "*cinghiale* couple" from a distance. We thought two brown cows were in the road. Then as we approached, Craig and I recognized them as being *cinghiale* (wild boar). They looked positively prehistoric. Craig stopped the car and killed the motor. We just stared at them in fascination. The male was bigger and quite dark, charcoal brown. The female was a more light brown. They had been enjoying a mud bath in all the mud churned up by the installation of the Algerian Pipeline. The male's low-slung haunches were caked with mud. He was leading the way, pausing to check for danger every few steps. He wasn't too bright because there was potential danger standing a few paces in front of his snout. The female politely followed his lead, although she seemed tense because she sensed danger. Eventually, they got across the pipeline ditch and trotted off stiff-legged into the forest.

Sometimes living in the middle of a hunting reserve has its moments. Last year, we saw two massive porcupines on the steepest part of our *Casanovalta* road. Their great quills rose up and shimmered in the headlights of our car. Then they ambled languorously off the road. Craig and I felt awestruck. The next day, we found long brown and white porcupine quills on the ground.

April 9

This weekend, I will do more work on the floors. Oh, how I have slaved on them. Then tomorrow, Craig and I will spend the day at a big Italian wedding.

I witnessed a charming scene just now framed by the small window in Craig's bedroom. Looking out the little window, I could see Craig accompanied by our dog Keshkek, taking the photos from our Christmas party to show the Ricci brothers who were working in the high field above *Casanovalta*. The handsome brothers, Gioli and Mauro, dark haired, bearded and mustached, were loading their tractor with a pile of *scopa* (Scottish broom) they had cut in the forest. I enjoyed seeing the country-friendly, manly sight. By the way, *scopa* was used for making rustic brooms. *Scopa* is the Italian word for broom.

Ah, bed—I brushed linseed oil on the dining room floor today, with crude oil—not cooked oil. I learned yesterday, from the mother of the groom, (a Pergine matron and the local bar keeper whose opinion I respect), that her tile man told her to use crude oil—because tile does not absorb cooked oil very well. (How painfully I have learned that lesson). She did her whole house perfectly. She felt sorry for me that I had used cooked oil—as I was told to do by our mason, our handyman, and every other person I've ever asked. I've been trying for years to figure out how to do the the tile floors at *Casanovalta*. Now we will see how crude linseed oil does. It doesn't seem to turn the tile too dark like the other. After the application of linseed oil, the final stage of floor perfection is adding a layer of wax. The living room looks elegant with its new coat of hand rubbed beeswax. I put on the wax—then Craig and I both rubbed and rubbed until the floor shone.

I stopped to pluck wild yellow primroses that were growing by the side of the *Casanovalta* road. The Pergine priest "doffed" his *chapeau* at me in a medieval manner. He was staring at my car as I drove down to deliver a message. We have no telephone yet. We've been waiting for one month since yesterday, when the poles and the lines were finally installed. When I waved at the priest, he ducked his head down, grabbed his curved hat by the crest, and walked on facing the ground with his hat raised in his outstretched hand. Italian priests have style. I wonder if my friendly greeting made him feel self-conscious?

April 10

It is just too early. Craig and I are up at the crack of dawn to get ready for the wedding. Everyone meets at the groom's house in Pergine, then drives to the church in Badia al Pino, the town of the bride. According to our *muratorio* Antonio, a three hour wedding will ensue, followed by an endless feast. The wedding will take place at the church in Badia al Pino and the wedding feast will be held in Pergine at our local *Le Cantine* restaurant. We have to get started this early with the wedding in order to finish in time for lunch. I wonder what the bride is feeling right now?

A few days ago when I took our wedding present over to the mother-in-law's house, she took me to see the hand embroidered, pink-sheeted wedding bed. This archaic ritual seems to be a part of the wedding ceremony. The bride and groom will be living with the groom's parents for awhile. If I were the bride, I think I'd be embarrassed. But no, a formal wedding photo of Bruna and Ivo sitting on their wedding bed was on display for all the world to see.

What a day. The wedding lunch lasted from noon until 4 p.m. At 9 a.m., Craig and I were among the first to arrive at the home of the groom. Craig had grabbed some biscuits before going out the door at home because we didn't know that there would be a wedding breakfast. No wedding guest should go hungry for even one minute.

We felt proud to be a part of the groom's Pergine car-parade driving to the village of his bride. Her parade arrived at the church the same moment ours did. Her car was bedecked with fresh yellow and white flowers. Her dress was flowing white with an under layer of yellow chiffon. She had yellow orchids in her hair, and she carried a bouquet of yellow orchids. For a country wedding this wasn't too shabby. Her family drove a BMW and her groom, Ivo, drove an Alfa Romeo. The bride's family have acres and acres of peach trees. Both families are hard working. Many Tuscans feel that they are born to do nothing but work, especially farmers. They rarely ever travel. They only spend their money on certain things, among them cars and weddings. I think the folks in these parts take pride in living modestly—but know secretly that they are very rich.

I felt startled by the difference between an American and an Italian wedding ceremony. The Italian ceremony seemed to lack dignity and felt chaotic. The photographers were everywhere with flood lights, movie cameras, and flash cameras. The groom, Ivo, went right into the church and stood at the altar. His bride, Bruna, came directly from her car and walked down the aisle on her father's arm. We, the audience, were still standing outside.

I saw Bruna's face, serious with concentration, and I felt empathy. We followed her in and found a place in the pews. Other people noisily milled in while the priest droned the mass into a microphone, certain that no one was listening. They weren't. The crowd chatted with one another and rubber-necked around to see who was there. I felt shocked by the lack of reverence and respect.

The priest said, "Far be it from me to say anything about the significance of marriage"—and then expounded unctuously on the topic for twenty minutes. I sensed a profound lack of rapport and communication between the priest and the congregation. I considered it hypocritical that anyone at all took communion. Impressionable young girls seemed keen on doing it. Because so many bodies walked about during the wedding ceremony, I had to be told when it was over.

Afterwards in the parking lot, the bride exuberantly kissed each and everyone there. I felt touched when she grabbed me in her arms, strong from picking peaches, and gave me a rib-cracking squeeze. She and Ivo kissed absolutely everyone.

Next, the whole wedding party formed one giant parade and drove back to Pergine arriving at *Le Cantine* restaurant where they were set up to serve a sit-down feast to one hundred and forty people. Seven cooks had been working for two days to prepare the wedding banquet.

This was the menu:

- *Antipasto*—crostini of liver or tomato, salami, prosciutto, hard eggs with basil, anchovy paste on bread, rice salad, peas and carrots salad, and seafood salad.
- *Pasta*—canneloni, fettucini with mushrooms, spinach ravioli, tortelini with meat sauce.
- *Pasto*—roasted wild boar's leg flamed, roast pork, chicken, lamb, pigeon, beef ribs, fried potatoes, peas, lettuce salad, and unlimited wine.
- *Dolce*—a seven tiered cake coated in chocolate, nuts, and flaky pastry. Fresh fruit cocktail, and *spumante* (sweet sparkling wine).
  (The groom's cake was a monster stuffed penis served on a platter).

I was amazed at how those people could eat. The bride and groom attacked their food with gusto. In between courses, the bride kissed everyone there yet another time. The groom, normally shy and reserved, held up his end as host in a manly fashion. The poor parents were flushed and faint with exhaustion, but smiled gamely. The bride, a hearty outgoing girl, smiled until her face was falling off. She posed for photos with almost everyone present before going in to eat. I heard her calling out in her husky voice, "*Fotografo, fotografo!*" (photographer, photographer), until her throat was raw.

After feasting, the bride and groom walked up the main street of Pergine with the wedding party following along behind them. The groom was escorting his bride to her new home. At that same moment, *I Musici,* our local band, was forming in the street to march and play a concert. Mass had just finished in the town church and the congregation was letting out. For the first time, the streets of Pergine seemed filled with every person who lived there. The band started playing and marching, and the church bells began chiming. What a grand finale it was to a magnificent wedding day.

Back home, Craig collapsed into bed for a nap. Only after touching up one of my linseed oiled floors, did I take a nap as well. If the oil isn't being absorbed, I spread it around before it dries. My spine and ribs ache and burn.

At dusk, I walked off the wedding feast with Keshkek and Muffin. The night seemed mild with only a slight chill. Muffin accompanied us the whole way in her own exotic fashion.

I was examining the progress on our terraces—and she, humorously, squeezed her whole body into a drainpipe, tail and all. I asked Keshkek, "Where is Muffin?" And he whined and pawed on the ground at the entrance to the pipe—then went around to the other end to sniff. Muffin got herself wedged inside the pipe and was only able to extract herself on the second try.

As we continued our walk, she ran up six trees in succession. She zoomed straight up the biggest oak tree, then headed straight down in several bouncy bounds, and then straight up another one several leaps away. It was as though her descent gave her the momentum to go up the next. I applauded her. She was so comical and seemed to have an enormous sense of humor. Muffin was showing off her new tree climbing skills since moving to the country. My mother's heart burst with pride over her and I felt deeply amused.

She continued to follow "Keshy" and me down the country road, very far for a cat to go on a walk, at one point losing us when her descent tangled her up in brambles. I heard her calling, "Meow! Meow!" Keshkek and I went back to help and show her the way back onto the road. Then I carried her for awhile, as her tree climbing was slowing us down and I wanted to dig up some wild violets before we lost the light. I found a patch or two in the moss and ferns under the trees in my favorite chestnut grove. At that point, Muffin overshot her mark because she speeded up a young tree and found herself balancing with "all four" on a springy twig. Coming down was the problem. She tried backing down with all 18 claws spiking like a lumber jack. I rushed over to place a supporting hand on her back, and lifted her down lovingly.

I was told today, that at the Pergine bar, a hunter spoke of a big white cat he'd seen in the forest. The hunter felt awestruck and said he had not killed her because she was so beautiful.

I think of Muffin as wearing a glowing shield of protection. We've also spread the word that a white cat lives at *Casanovalta* who is very much loved. Craig and I are always careful of Keshkek and Muffin, even when it is not hunting season. Fortunately, the new season is not open yet.

I just made myself nervous. I went to the kitchen door and called and called out into the dark night for Muffin to come in from her hunting and go to bed. When she didn't come right away, I began ringing the brass bell mounted on the wall by the kitchen entry, very loudly. She's in.

April 11

I'm at peace with my home, husband, and mason. Soft green is sprouting on the willow trees and we three are working harmoniously together. Antonio blew it all out in drunken debauchery for three days over Easter with his brothers, who were visiting from Abruzzo. Now he is subdued—and even slightly kind. We are finishing the cabinet bases in the lower bathroom, which was a former sheep stall.

I find huge satisfaction in putting clothes to dry on the clothesline stretching across my front yard, claimed from the stinging nettles. There is some sunshine. I potted violets.

April 12

The gravel truck is coming and going and dumping sand under my clothesline. Antonio is having his cement mixer delivered today. I feel frustrated. The wind is howling but the sky remains clear.

Earlier today I wrote in my journal, "I feel fat and have decided I hate my hair. I'm not feeling centered. I could scream." I did.

A phantom man from SIP, *Società Idroelettrica Piemontese*, (Piedmont Hydroelectric Company) passed by—a red-shirted body walking by our house. I thought it could possibly be a rude hunter. But no, it was someone from the phone company—because I glanced outside to see the telephone truck departing down the road. But why didn't they come inside and install our phone? Oh, how I wish we had a telephone.

Craig and I have learned that no Italian man ever makes a mistake. (One thought he did once—but he was wrong).

I often feel that Antonio takes out his frustration on me because he sees me as weaker than himself. Today, the width of the bathroom countertop—relative to the newly made plaster base—was too narrow for the sink basin and the faucets to fit. There needed to be sufficient space for the faucet holes to be cut in the marble countertop. Craig and Antonio had discussed this issue for half-an-hour before proceeding with the work. Antonio had assured Craig there was "no problem," (his favorite expression). But Antonio had forgotten to calculate for a metal support bar which had to be fitted into the space—thus ruination. Antonio ranted at me, demanding to know what we should do for a solution. I tried to reason it out—not wanting to disturb Craig, who was napping. I asked why hadn't measurements been reasoned out before? Antonio claimed that Craig had wanted it this way—ha. Fortunately, Craig arose in time to suggest the solution of putting the faucets on the side—not perfect, but better than ripping out the wall or rebuilding a new plaster base. No matter how hard we try, our house is full of strange compromises. It's a real peasant built house.

I mellowed towards Antonio when he complimented the beauty of the floors I crude-oiled today, *"La piastrella è bella."* (The tile is beautiful). My wrists ache.

My animals looked so cute going right to their temporary beds in the bathroom tonight. Keshkek curled up on his round red pad which I had I tossed on the floor in front of the radiator, and Muffin nestled on Craig's red sweatshirt, which covered his dark socks in his sock drawer. Craig's sock drawer happens to be sitting on top of the bidet because I'm currently oiling his bedroom floor.

April 13

In the evening, when Craig drove Antonio down the hill, I went downstairs to admire the work they'd been doing all day on the lower bathroom. To my horror, I saw that the opening I had designed—to be able to sit down at the vanity area—was filled in with bricks and cement. The cement was getting harder by the minute. My architectural drawings were lying in a pile nearby—unnoticed. I gave the bricks a mighty kick with my wooden shoes and savagely clawed at the cement with a pick-ax until I had pulled it all apart. Thank God, I caught the mistake in time. I couldn't believe that my architect husband and trusted mason had done that. The design imitated the upstairs bathroom. What could they have been thinking?

When Craig came home I told him, "There was a crisis—but I fixed it with a pick-ax." He looked startled. I took him downstairs and asked, "Do you see anything different?" He didn't notice a thing.

April 14

I'd like to be able to give my needs first priority for a change. I have trouble doing that. I can say it—but I can't do it.

I dreamt last night that I have only a few pages left in this journal and a great deal to say in the remaining space. I believe in journal writing and have always kept one of some kind. It helps me feel more in touch with myself.

I picked purple daisies today.

April 15

What a wretched night—my muscles were too tense for me to sleep well—or to feel rested. I kept waking up from a repetitious dream where big bushy-tailed rats kept dashing about in the kitchen. They kept coming up through broken tiles in the floor. I kept dreaming about trying to wake up but feeling too exhausted to do so. Then I dreamt that Craig came stumbling into my room saying that he had a cold and couldn't go to get Antonio—I would have to do it. But I couldn't handle it because I simply could not wake up.

At last, I have awakened—to work. My animals rushed in to kiss me, as they do almost every morning. Craig is bringing me coffee, as he does almost every morning.

This was a good day's work. I hope I don't dream about rats tonight.

April 16

What's fair is fair. "Keshy" is whining at the bathroom door and awakening me. I keep trying to sleep and leave him in the bathroom, but he is persistent. Since Craig hasn't awakened, I know he is sleeping in for a change. So I get up to let the animals out of the bathroom and take them outside to pee. Actually, we all enjoyed peeing outside. It is a fine spring morning and I take a walk in my nightdress, not feeling too chilled, and appreciate all the beautiful buds. Even the blackberry brambles seem pretty with their tiny white flowers.

Coming back inside the kitchen, I notice that it is 7:30 a.m.—the hour when Keshkek was accustomed to going down the hill to pick up Antonio. But it's Saturday—thank God.

Yesterday, I covered Craig's bedroom floor with self-shining wax—because rubbing every floor with beeswax is just too much. It looks pretty good. I had to work the wax into the rough surface of the tile with a brush, but I'm satisfied with the results.

In an act of desperation, I cut my own hair today—never a wise move. It has holes in it but approaches a sort of casual style. I can truthfully say I've outgrown "Alice in Wonderland" and have become "Ringo Starr."

April 18

Muffin sits on a kitchen stool exuding peaceful vibes while all around her is a frantic scurry. I have finished waxing the dining room floor. It's a jewel. It looks like glazed terra cotta. My back is racked with pain. Craig is tidying the messiest room, which creates a furor in the kitchen. So, I've gone out to my favorite corner of the terrace to find a quiet place to write.

One of the more endearing qualities about Italy are the simple country folk. Long ago, we befriended an elderly couple, Armando and Rina Mateucci, who were general workers and guardians at the *Montelucci* winery, located a little way down the hill from *Casanovalta*. We saw quite a bit of them in the early days of our restoration project. The husband, Armando, is petite and wiry, whereas his wife, Rina, is twice his size. But she is bent over double because of her bad back—and poor medical attention. She always has a broad smile on her face, more like a grimace—almost like smiling in the face of pain. She adores her small husband and protects him fiercely. She carries twice the load of firewood so he doesn't have to. She says defensively, *"Armando è piccolo!"* (Armando is little).

Rina Mateucci is the woman who helped me wash fifty plus years of grime off the *Casanovalta* kitchen floor. She and her husband, Armando, would always offer us their good *Vinsanto* every time we passed by. But this year, we've been so self-involved we've only seen them a few times. Recently, Craig drove Armando up the hill. He had been shopping in Pergine because Rina had been in the hospital. I really meant to pass by with cookies, but never seemed to find the time.

So this evening, when I saw Rina standing on the road at the entrance to the *Fattoria Montelucci* (Montelucci Farm), I slammed on the brakes and went running to embrace her. I asked about her operation and said how sorry I was not to have come visiting sooner. Just seconds before seeing Rina, I had been thinking of her strongly. She took me down to the house to see Armando. They offered me *Vinsanto* (sweet Tuscan dessert wine). Armando commented that he had seen my car pass by two and one-half hours before and that he had mentioned to the *Fattore* (director of the winery) that they never saw us anymore. The director had told Armando, "They have not forgotten you. They're probably just busy." I heartily reassured Armando that we thought of them quite often. "We truly have not forgotten you." I offered my condolences for his brother who had died during the winter. Armando, who had been held as a prisoner of war in Australia, said in English, "A good man." I said, "Yes, your brother was a good man." "Thank you," Armando replied humbly. Then Armando fetched his wheelbarrow and helped me cart away six sacks of trash, that I had forgotten to dump and had left in the back of the car. These were good old friends.

Back home, Craig prepared a tasty dinner of salmon patties—bless his heart. He's been feeling sad today over the sudden death of Carlton Winslow, the famous professor (*"professore"*) from Cal Poly San Luis Obispo, who had rented our house last winter. He made many friends in Pergine and was well loved by the locals. They admiringly referred to him as *"il professore."* He had planned on returning in June. Antonio felt deeply sad too. The professor and *i studenti* (the students) were often on his doorstep last year. Antonio had taken them under his wing and felt proud to know them. He reminisced fondly of *"i studenti."* We all thought of Carleton today.

April 19

The dining room floor has become a shrine. We take our shoes off to walk across it.

April 20

I lie in bed thinking about cat anatomy and how amazing it is—Muffin's in particular. She seems to like it when I get a good grip on her "armpits" and hold her with her body dangling down. She goes limp and resembles a slinky toy. I say to her, "You're stretchy like E.T.," as she distends what seems like twice her body length. Then in contrast, this soft, squishy kitty becomes an electric whip during the hunt. Yesterday, I saw her do a "death dance"—what seemed like an ancient encoded ritual. The only other time I ever saw another cat do this was a Bengal tiger at the circus. Muffin was hunting what looked like a snake, but turned out to be a lizard with its jaws wide open. Muffin's spine became so rigid that her back arched into a V. Then to my astonishment, she rose on her hind legs, her front paws in tuck position and her tail pulled up —and leaped straight up into the air landing slightly to the right on her hind legs. She balanced on her hind legs, body upright, and took a high leap to the left before dropping down onto the "snake." Muffin was strutting her stuff because she knew I was watching. I'll bet ancient Angora cats were mighty hunters. It's no wonder Muffin goes on sleeping binges. What energy she must consume to perform such extraordinary feats of athleticism and instinctive hunting skill.

This recent dialog with intruders, who interloped onto our property last Sunday, strikes me as extremely amusing. I have the impression that Tuscans are curious, extremely conversational, and obsessed with procreation.

Because Craig was so annoyed with the family of *contadine* (country folk) who felt they had the right to walk on our property, picnic on a planted field of *erba medica* (alfalfa), and stare down at our house—I went up to let them know they were intruding on private land.

The intruders became aggressive. I stood my ground. And in the end, we all became good friends.

The exchange began like this—with them demanding to know, "Is this your land?"

Me: "Yes it is."

Them: "We're relatives of Ricci."

Me: "We give the use of our land to Ricci to farm."

Them: "How much land have you got?"

Me: "2 ½ *ettari* (hectares).

Them: "Whose land is that?" The intruders pointed further up the hill.

Me: "Zaccheo. He uses it for his cattle."

Them: "Well, why does the road pass by here?"

Me: "It's an access road for farm machinery for Zaccheo, Ricci, and Ellwood."

Them: "You should put up private property signs."

Me: "We did. They're on the road. Didn't you see them?"

Them: "You should put up pillars and a chain at your entrance."

Me: "We did. Didn't you see the red pillars of steel on the road? The hunters cut the chain."

Them: "You should put stone pillars to the entrance of your driveway and a chain to close the road."

Me: "We will when we can. The *muratore* must finish the terraces first."

Them: "Do you live here alone?"

Me: "No, with my husband."

Them: "Where is he?"

Me: "In the house."

Them: "Do you have any children?"

Me: "No."

Them: "You don't have any children?"

Me: "No."

Them: "Why don't you have any children?"

Me: "Because I'm not Italian."

Them: "Do you plan on having any children?"

Me: "Not yet."

Them: "Well, you're young yet. Are you an American?"

Me: "Yes."

Boy: " Why does your car have an Arezzo plate?"

Me: "Because we live in the district of Arezzo. Our phone number has an Arezzo prefix as well."

Them: "Is that your dog?"

Me: "Yes."

Them: "He's a *bastardo?*" (neutered).

Me: "Yes. He's a *bastardo* and a California sport dog." I showed the boy how Keshkek could play "stick"—leaping high in the air to catch and retrieve a tossed stick. Everyone was amazed and delighted.

Me: "I have a big, white cat too."

Them: "Can she have a litter?"

Me: "No. She's neutered."

Them: "Neutered?"

Me: "Yes. I brought my dog and cat to Italy on an airplane."

Them: "Did you pay for them to come over on the airplane?"

Me: "Yes."

Them: "You paid?"

Me: "Right."

Them: "Your willow trees got all broken from the ice and wind."

Me: "Yes, they did."

Them: "May we come sometime to look for mushrooms in the forest?"

Me: "I give you my permission. *Buona sera.*" (Good evening).

Today is one of those days that's worth the price we've paid. It is a hot, glorious spring day. I sit in my vantage point corner on the terrace wall writing in my journal. I hear the gentle scraping sound of Antonio spreading plaster. I can't get up. The sun is heaven. Keshkek stretches his freshly washed body beside me. I smell that clean dog scent. I'm getting my batteries charged. I'm also getting sunburned.

At nine o'clock last night, there was a perfect half moon. A faint color was left in the sky and misty stars began making Persian crosses. An owl hooted and other creatures made indefinable night noises. Mufffin and Keshkek trotted on the forest path beside me with the warm, moist air ruffling their fur. Spring has finally arrived.

May 12

The telephone was installed—but not connected. "Metaphysical SIP" welled up out of the blue—fortunately finding Craig at home. He was hauling rock from the Algerian pipeline gash to our house for the terraces. We are using the actual rock from the region to build our terrace walls in the back of the house. The color matches our house perfectly, beautiful ochre colored stone. If the pipeline had not come through, we would not have found sufficient rock with which to complete our terrace walls.

With some forceful persuasion on his part, Craig convinced the SIP technician to install the phone positioned how he liked it—with the cord coming out from a less visible source inside the kitchen cabinet.

Just to tantalize us, the phone sits perkily on our kitchen countertop just as it was meant to do. But there is no dial tone. We are not yet connected to *la linea centrale* (the central line). This will not happen until we have paid for the total installation of the phone. Of course in all this while, we have never received a finalized bill or any written form of communication from SIP whatsoever.

May 13

Craig and I, intrepid warriors, went to SIP headquarters in Arezzo this morning. The office personnel seemed startled, even befuddled, by our appearance. They kept asking repeatedly, "Do you have the telephone? Were you told to come here to pay? You have the lines? And you say you have the telephone? You've come to ask a question? You say you want to pay your bill?"

Frantic calling to the technicians and to other SIP offices to get the final tally ensued—apparently, there was no central computer which stored the data. At last, Craig wrote a check for one million, nine hundred eighty-four thousand lire—and we officially became the proud owners of an Italian telephone. I kept asking when we could have the connection to la linea centrale. But they were vague about that. The office manager, Signor Zacchi, offered us a "Roman promise." He said, "You can have the phone connected this very day, if a squad of technicians are in the area. If not, then on Monday—or sometime thereafter." Hmm, I hope somebody remembers to connect us.

A letter arrived today from my Los Angeles best friend, Mary Collins. I wrote a fifteen page letter in response.

No telephone connection today.

May 19

What a magical time of day. The sun is setting over the valley and the *rondini* (swallows) are back, flying by the eaves of the house like mini-jet bombers picking off mosquitos in the twilight sky. The white *Maremma* cattle were herded to their summer pasture above our house this morning and are lowing. The church bells are ringing in the village church below. In the sky above, a perfect half-moon rests delicately. My heart is filled with gratitude and relief. I said to Muffin and Keshkek, "God bless you both. We have survived the winter."

Never underestimate the power (muscle power that is) of an Italian woman. My good hearted new maid, Paola, breezed in this afternoon with two female friends. The women were dressed for the fields wearing colorful smock covered dresses and cotton bandanas on their heads. Each woman wielded a sharp scythe in her right hand. They attacked our overgrown grounds with humor and gusto. I gave orders, fetched cups of water, and attempted to use a scythe myself. Antonio, who witnessed this impressive scene joked rather jealously that today, "I wore the stripes." I had all the assistants and he had none.

Those women really did a job on the stinging nettles which surrounded the house. We all got skin burns. I was extremely impressed with their speed and skill, far superior to mine. One of the women said her husband had lived at *Casanovalta* as a child. That felt like such an important piece of history to me. I gave them all a tour of the house at the end of the day. Paola was an old hand by now, but the other two looked rather in awe. They exclaimed, *"Complimenti!"* (Well done). Paola said I was *"brava"* for my work on the floors.

May 24 (Eleven days later)

"Bring, bring!" Our day began with the jolly ringing of our telephone. I was the first to answer it. A voice on the other end of the line said, "È SIP. Il telefono è pronto. Funziona." (It is SIP. The telephone is ready. It functions). I said, *"Bravo. Grazie. Buongiorno."* At long last. We called Jeffrey Smart in celebration. Jeffrey has been calling all morning to let us practice answering the telephone and to accustom us to the sound—for joy.

May 25

Our toil on the house goes on and on. I oiled the entire "music room" floor, giving it a second coat in one day. Yesterday, Craig and I both oiled the downstairs guest suite. Today, Antonio is painting the walls of the "garden room" white. He is in a nasty mood because he was forced to stop working on the terraces. Due to insufficient old tile, we needed to mix a pattern of old and new tile together, which we would use to cap the terrace walls. The tile truck was late on delivery of the new tile because it couldn't pass on the Montelucci road—because the Algerian pipeline had dug it in two. I went to meet the truck on the Civitella road, a very treacherous country road, and lead it to the opposite entrance of our house. The new batch of tile is more pale in color—which threw Antonio into a rage. This behavior seems strange to me because these are our terraces. But I think Antonio is tired from overworking and needs to blow off steam. He said he wasn't going to come to work the following Monday unless he has an assistant. He really got himself worked up over that one. I found this odd as well because Antonio never works with an assistant. Craig offered to pay for an assistant if Antonio could find one.

May 26
Antonio came to work today with no assistant—and was just barely civil.

May 28
Craig has gone to buy flowers, which is the best part of fixing up the house. Antonio maintains a perfect balance between being a remarkable human being and a nasty shit.

I waxed the "music room," our second living room and the largest room in the house, until 3 a.m. last night when I ran out of wax. Waxing is the ultimate finishing touch. I'm disappointed in the way it looks in contrast to its other half—the smaller living room which still has its original tile. The surface is too new and smooth looking.

This day turned out far better than I had anticipated. I put in a huge work effort and the end is in sight. The "garden room" is a joyful place now instead of being a junk heap—and at this very moment I have finally finished waxing the "music room."

Telephones don't work in Italy when it rains. In the four days we have had the telephone, Craig has received four calls from America. I just got my first special call, a ring to say, "Hello," from my American friend, Anne Francorsi, married to an Italian from Venice and Rome. Her son, Cesare Domenico, celebrated his first birthday today. She doesn't know if she can come for an overnight visit because her Italian husband must be fed his lunch everyday.

May 31
Today I am "resting on my laurels." Craig's oldest son, Jeff, arrived from California yesterday for a visit. He was greeted by a heavenly house full of spring flowers and every surface gleaming. That same afternoon, a writer for *Architectural Digest* photographed the house to show his

editor. It has been Craig's long held fantasy, the dream of having our house published. We have come a long way.

It is a joy to open our morning windows to fields of wildflowers and tender sunlight. To be able to bask in the sun on the terraces is a sybaritic delight. We toiled to wrest those terraces from the resistant earth. With the help of the Algerian Pipeline we put a mighty dent in it. Craig and I hauled in every single rock.

June 1

Muffin reclines in the shady, tall grass of the high meadow. A breeze ruffles her long fur. She reminds me of a white rose.

Antonio returned to work on the terraces today mellowed from his three day *festa* (party). He shared raw lima beans from his garden and a slice of cheese with me. We're back to normal. Later in the day, he told me the reason he *felt rabbia* (rage). It was because the new tiles that had been delivered were a different color from the previous ones. It really bothered him that the terraces would not look perfect. He wanted it all to look beautifully rose colored and antique. Although he is quite human and makes mistakes like the rest of us, I do give Antonio credit for his standards. I also think he's making excuses for himself.

June 2

The studio terrace and lower terrace walls are finished. They look magnificent. The cement caps to the stone walls look clean and natural. I feel very happy about them. It is a major achievement for all of us— Antonio included—especially Antonio.

Antonio did a gentle act at the *"Sagra di Prosciutto"* (ham festival) in Pergine on Sunday. Each village has some form of food that they produce and celebrate annually. We were sitting together at a table eating *salsiccia* (sausage) and *bruschetta* (garlicky toasted bread with olive oil) when Antonio called out, *"C'è la mia ragazza!"* (There's my girlfriend). He swept up a little girl and sat her on his lap. She had Down's Syndrome. The little girl was obviously smitten with Antonio and delighted to be with him. She sat peacefully in his lap—completely at home. He complimented her pretty dress and polished fingernails. Then he graciously gave her a taste of his beer. Antonio explained to me and Craig, *"Credo nei bambini"* (I believe in children).

Keshkek gallantly chased a wild boar off our property today. He's our protector.

June 8

Craig and his son have gone off to the sea, la *Maremma Toscana* (Tuscany at the Maremma). It seemed important to me for them to share some special time together. At home alone with my animals, I'm hauling water from the ancient cistern which still provides water. I've been drawing buckets up by hand. There seems to be a water shortage. I'm thinking there could be some sort of malfunction in the reserve tank. I will call the plumber. I can call the plumber now because our telephone has been repaired. It was out for two and a-half days because a tree branch was touching our single line somewhere in the forest. I am here with no car, no water, and as of yesterday, no telephone. However, I have found *Casanovalta* and its setting a delight to my physical senses; smell, touch, sight —and also, there is a sense of almost no sound.

As I drew water from the cistern, I had a satisfying "primordial" image of my own farm stock heritage. Pulling the rock away from the well in the high field with sun streaming across the dry wheat, feeling the coolness of the water drawn up by bucket on a rope, and carrying the heavy, full buckets across the hot fields felt both ancient and familiar to me. I had a sensation of being present in the moment yet connected to the past as well. The water in the bucket was so cool and inviting that I washed my face and dipped my hands and feet in it. Feeling generous, I gave the new gardenia on our porch a drink of the precious water. The gardenia sweetens our entry. I'm feeling in close contact with the elements of air, water, sun, and earth finding comfort in my senses.

I promised my dog a walk and we managed to catch the sunset. We celebrated it the entire length of our country walk as we watched it set across the hayfield, which made an ocean of golden mown hay. And so we come to the close of our earthly and ethereal day. Again, I feel a sense of contentment as I sit on the porch enjoying the cool of the evening.

June 10

All systems have been repaired—and Antonio deserves to be shot. Due to his spiteful temperament on Tuesday, he left the rubber hose running full blast. Prior to that, he had been filling a leaky can with water for his cement. He had been so busy resenting us that he forgot to turn off the water. So for two days and two nights the hose has been running full blast and our precious water reserve has been exhausted.

I finally called the plumber when the semi-full reserve tank emptied mysteriously after the water pressure was finally high enough to bring water out of the taps. This condition would last for five minutes and then the water pressure would mysteriously disappear. Then I would discover that the reserve tank was empty again.

The plumber pronounced a *perdita* (leak) in the lines to the house. He asked if there were any humid walls. I said, "No, we just had new humidity walls built." Finding the *perdita* meant that we might have to externally dig up the entire outside water lines, or tear up the walls and floors of the house to find the leak. I was dying a thousand deaths.

Rolando began poking about the yard and around the terraces. He asked about the new stone terrace and who was our *muratore*? I said, "Antonio of Pergine." Rolando followed his fox-like nose to a large water container and peered inside. There was a great wetness on the ground around it. He asked, "What is this?" I said, "Oh, that's just a container that leaks." His eyes lighted on the rubber hose entering the container and exclaimed, "No it isn't!" He rushed to the water spigot and turned it off with a flourish. After that, the water pressure went up in seconds and water again flowed from the taps. I was ecstatic with relief.

Ironically, I've been planning the dinner I will cook for Antonio and his family on Saturday. I hope to redeem my reputation in the kitchen somewhat—and Antonio needs to redeem his good standing with me.

The on-going saga of my relationship with Antonio amuses and frustrates me. We are clearly the opposite of each other, with the good and the bad of each side represented. Sometimes we dislike each other and at other times we experience respect, and occasional admiration—and maybe even deep down—genuine affection. However, he totally denied leaving the water tap on.

June 12

The dinner party for Antonio and his wife, Margherita, was a success. I served vermouth cassis cocktails to start. The drinks were accompanied by Mexican nachos. This seemed to be a big hit. Then I served wok chicken with fried rice. Margherita considered this dish to be "Arabian." She complimented my cooking. I asked my nemesis, "I'm not so *cattiva* (wicked) after all?" Antonio winked slyly, "No, just a *vagabonda*." Humph, he still considers me to be a vagabond. After cookies and ice cream, Craig gave Antonio a small replica Etruscan statue and his wife a gardenia. He knows how to be a gracious host and gallant to the ladies.

June 13, 1983

White moths flutter amongst the snowy white field flowers as I sit dreamily in the shade of the front porch with my dog and cat drowsing nearby. A sunny hay field lies above my house and a shadowy valley below. I think it is unique to live in a place where no cars pass by. The Ricci brothers bundled hay today in the high field. Now we have haystacks dotting the landscape. Craig and I took photos of each other standing beside the haystacks with pitchforks in our hands. We're such ridiculous city slickers.

June 15

I'm sitting on a sunny log and counting the hay bails in the field. White cows and calves in the next field seem deep in meditation as they chew their cuds. Similar to the swallows returning to Capistrano, we know it is springtime when the white cattle return to the fields above *Casanovalta*.

Last night, Muffin leaped up from her resting place to chase a giant black bat that shockingly started flying around inside the living room. I screamed and put a book over my head. She didn't catch it.

June 18

The telephone is having a nervous "tinkling attack" because it's raining. It just can't handle a bit of rain. So far it has broken down completely every time it rains. SIP repairmen have a guaranteed job for life.

It is my belief that Italy is a nation which has perfected the art of lying. *"Bugiardo"* (liar) is a word people use with a twinkle in their eye and a sly wink. From Naples to Milan the art of lying is practiced daily with subtle refinements. Some individuals have achieved a mastery level. I ought to know—having been on the receiving end of it many times.

I'm reading a homey book on growing herbs, drinking coffee, and eating homemade oatmeal cookies. Vivaldi and Bach fill the house with balanced tones. Cozy. The life at *Casanovalta* can be sweet if I pause to enjoy it. I wonder if life might be fine with Craig back to painting and me growing herbs, and—with the deepest tenderness—a baby? We shall see.

June 19

I've resigned myself to the way Antonio has built our exterior stairway, with a busy rock lip on each tread. The stairway connects the upper and lower rear terraces. I wanted to see just a strong and simple rock mass. But instead, I think it looks contemporary and ordinary. That one slipped past our overseeing.

Keshkek and I went for a walk in the rain—since it was our ritual walk time at the high tea hour. To my wonderment, I found wild strawberries in full fruit. Never have I tasted a more beautiful flavor. The tiny berries covered with droplets of rain were robust with a mystical, herb-like, perfumed, richly sweet flavor. Something had attracted me—truly drew me—to a mossy bank of land by the side of my country hill-forest road. My thought process went like this, "I wonder if there are any edible herbs here, like wild parsley, that I could transplant? Perhaps there is a plant with a pretty leaf. Oh, those are pretty leaves—my God!" It was then I saw the tiny red fruit under the light green leaves. I lay down the flowers I was carrying to cram the almost indescribably delicious fruit into my mouth. They were "God's jujubes."

June 20

Late June is cherry season in dear old *Italia*—cherries and strawberries— such luscious fruit. This has been an uncommonly beautiful day, a sparkling treasure from beginning to end.

At dinnertime, I went to find the wild strawberries again. I dug one up and noticed that it grew in shale and leafy-bark soil. So I dug up some shale and bark for it to have in its pot. Now, I have wild strawberries and wild violets growing in the shade of our front porch. Looking out the kitchen door I see gardenias, violets, strawberries, basil, mint, green onions, dill, cilantro, and geraniums growing in pots on the front steps and porch. In addition, there's an antique olive tree ladder, a wooden hay rake, a long-handled copper pan, an old heather broom, a woodpile stacked against the far wall, and a wicker chair. Casanovalta feels like home.

Recipes from Casanovalta

THESE SIMPLE, EVERYDAY RECIPES BRING YOU the flavors and feeling of life at our Tuscan farmhouse. The ingredients came from the land around us—dandelion greens foraged from the meadow, chestnuts found under my favorite tree, and blackberries gathered along our country lane.

Enjoy a taste of *Casanovalta's* rustic and nourishing cuisine!

Bruschetta

Rake hot coals forward on the hearth of the kitchen fireplace.

Place thick slices of freshly cut country bread on a grill
set over the embers.

Toast until golden and crisp, with just a hint of char.

Rub each slice with a clove of fresh garlic, releasing its bold aroma
into the bread.

Drizzle generously with just-pressed, emerald-green Tuscan
virgin olive oil.

Best enjoyed immediately while warm.

Wild Greens Salad

Gather wild dandelion and arugula greens from the front yard,
their leaves still moist from the morning dew.

Wash well and spin dry.

Toss with robust Tuscan olive oil and a pinch of coarse sea salt
from the Maremma.

Serve simply, allowing the peppery greens to shine.

Grilled Pork Chops

Buy *baciole di maiale* from the local butcher—thick-cut pork chops full of flavor.

Season generously with rosemary from the garden, pressed garlic, a sprinkle of sea salt, and a twist of black pepper

Grill over the fireplace coals until beautifully browned and sizzling.

Drizzle with a touch of olive oil before serving.

Pair with Wild Greens, Bruschetta, and a chilled glass of Pinot Grigio.

Fennel Salad

Select fat *feminine* (*femminile*) fennel bulbs, round and fragrant, and not the skinnier (*maschile*), male fennel bulbs.

Slice the *finocchio* paper-thin.

Drizzle with excellent Tuscan virgin olive oil.

Finish with freshly ground black pepper for a crisp, refreshing bite.

That is all—simple and perfect.

Blackberry Cobbler

Pick wild blackberries from the roadside, eating as many as possible before gathering enough for baking.

In a deep ceramic dish, toss the berries with 1/2 cup of sugar, letting them release their juices.

Cover with a soft Bisquick dough, made according to instructions on the box.

Bake until the pastry is golden brown, and the berries bubble beneath in a thick, fragrant syrup.

A favorite with house guests—especially when served warm with fresh cream.

Fig Jam

Gather fresh Pergine Valdarno figs from the neighbor's tree, their skins nearly bursting with ripeness.

Quarter the figs and place them in a heavy stainless steel pot.

Add just enough water to cover and a generous amount of sugar.

Stir in fragrant slivers of lemon peel.

Simmer until thick and glossy, the scent of caramelized figs filling the kitchen.

Spread on rough country bread for the perfect rustic breakfast.

Casanovalta "Stuck in a Snowstorm" Salad

Boil small white potatoes in their jackets until just tender.
Once cooled, slice them thinly.

Toss with flaky canned tuna, heaps of chopped parsley,
and a handful of capers.

Add minced scallions, and finely diced sweet-and-sour pickles
for brightness.

Season with sea salt and a pinch of red pepper flakes.

Dress with bold Tuscan olive oil and a splash of red wine vinegar.

See? You *did* have something to eat in the house.

Roasted Chestnuts

Gather wild chestnuts from under the full-crested tree in the forest
during the month of October when the air holds the first chill.

Nestle them into the fireplace coals and roast until their sweet, nutty
aroma fills the room, and their skins turn toasty brown.

Peel with care—the steamy nut meat can be hot, but the reward
is worth it.

Best enjoyed with good company.

Caprese Salad

Harvest sun-ripe tomatoes, heavy on the vine and bursting with flavor.

Pick fresh basil from the kitchen window pot.

Cut thick slices of tomato, seasoning each round with salt and pepper.

On a large platter, layer the tomatoes with rounds of creamy *mozzarella da bufala*, (made from *Toscana Maremma* water buffalo milk).

Scatter slivers of fresh basil over the top.

Drizzle with Tuscan olive oil and a few drops of *Aceto Balsamico di Modena*.

Pairs beautifully with a glass of Chianti Putto, our local wine.

Postscript

LESSONS LEARNED

I GAVE CASANOVALTA MY ENTIRE LIFE force—my youthful energy and creativity, my heart and soul—all throughout my 30s. In the end, at 40, I walked away. Yet the smells, flavors, and quality of life from that time in Tuscany will forever be a part of me. Each time I catch the scent of burning firewood, or the aroma of roasting chestnuts on charcoal, or the intoxicating bouquet of wild herbs on a dry wind, I think of *Casanovalta.*

The lessons in resilience I learned continue to serve me well, as do the trust and sense of possibility I developed while transforming a Renaissance-era ruin into a living, breathing home. I had no doubt I could do it, and I did.

Making my home now in Mexico, I find the flexibility I cultivated in Tuscany continues to shape my daily life. The tolerance and perseverance I developed while restoring *Casanovalta* help me navigate the day to day challenges of life here; whether it's a transformer exploding into flames and plunging the neighborhood into darkness, or our cobblestone street washing away in a heavy rain.

Mexico's vibrant colors and aliveness, and the lilt of the language, all remind me of Italy. I appreciate the spontaneity of the people, their way of going with the flow—not pushing against the river. Life can be tough, but if we band together with goodwill and humor, we'll manage.

As I learned at *Casanovalta*, it really doesn't help to worry all the time. I recall the early days of the restoration when we faced countless hurdles; missing doors and windows, unreliable plumbers, inadequate heating, and no running water—to name a few. Each challenge seemed insurmountable at the time, yet we found a way through. That experience taught me that persistence, not worry, is what moves mountains. And as my teacher, the venerable Baba Bedi once said, "When you trust your potential and move in the direction appropriate for you, *there are no obstacles—they have a way of vanishing.*"

San Miguel de Allende, Mexico 2025

Acknowledgments

THEY SAY IT TAKES A VILLAGE to raise a child—and I think it takes a village to make a book. I feel so grateful that the village I live in is San Miguel de Allende, which overflows with gifted people—some of whom I'm honored to call my friends. It has been my dream of a lifetime to write this book—and now, after being given the initial inspiration by Gabriele Cirami and Roberto Zancan, with the extraordinary support of my cherished friends and family, I have finally been able to make that dream come true.

In particular, I'd like to thank my dear friend and "art director," Sheridan Sansegundo, who said, "All you needed was a little bit of encouragement" to get started on my book—and to feel that I could do it. Sheridan gave me that encouragement—as well as her expert editing eye, impeccable sense of beauty and design, and her infinite good taste. We discussed how to give my book a form, designed its original structure, and the overarching concept of *CASANOVALTA*.

Another one of these very talented San Miguel people is Susan Fassberg ("Sooz"), who is my incomparable "editorial assist." I thank Sooz for being such a brilliant wordsmith and master technician. Your sensory descriptions and charming turns of phrase are pure delight. You were so generous to share your genius with me. I could not have made this book without you.

I give abundant thanks to my beloved sister, Brenda, who was witness to the early days, (and even drank coffee with me at the table set up on the sunny gravel driveway in front of *Casanovalta),* and so had the direct experience of being there. Thank you for your heartfelt support—and all the whimsical and wonderful watercolors which grace this book. I appreciate your enthusiasm, and for painting your heart out.

With her delicate hand, my friend of a lifetime, Claire Ryle Garrison, has brought the recipe section alive with her graceful botanical drawings. Her steady encouragement and subtle editing have kept my feet firmly on the path all along the way. Words cannot express my gratitude.

Others in my creative and talented San Miguel team include my friend Margaret Nash whose critical eye and wise words—and sometimes provocative challenge—have all been enormously helpful, and my dear friend Ellen Maria Vertommen whose enthusiastic and insightful comments have inspired me. My architect and "artist's artist" friend, Kassie Dummett, conferred with me on the subtleties of color selection and spatial values for my cover design; and Mary Jane Miller took me under her wing and told me how to produce a book— muchísimas gracias. I'd also like to thank my new friend and graphic designer, Claudia Castillo, whose patience and artistic eye helped me Photoshop the old photos and restore them to new life, plus interpreted my vision for the cover design beautifully. Finally, I want to express great gratitude to Mary Meade, the marvelous graphic designer who has skillfully and artfully put this book into form. How can I thank you all enough?

As this long-cherished dream of mine becomes a reality, all I can say is that my heart is overflowing with gratitude.

Bibliography

Jackson, Neil. *California Modern: The Architecture of Craig Ellwood*. New York: Princeton Architectural Press, 2003.

Boyd, Michael, ed. *Making LA Modern: Craig Ellwood–Myth/Man/Designer*. New York: Rizzoli, 2018.

Zancan, Roberto, ed. *Altre Case Come Me: Intellettuali e Spazio Domestico in Italia/ Intellectuels et Crise de l'Espace Domestique en Italie*. Brussels: ESA–Saint-Luc, 2022.

About the Author

Before moving to Italy with architect and painter Craig Ellwood, Anita Eubank spent her 20s performing as an actress, singer, and model in New York and Hollywood. In her 30s, she and Craig undertook the ambitious restoration of a Renaissance-era farmhouse in Tuscany.

While living in Italy, Anita completed her degree in psychology and produced *The First International Expressive Therapy Conference*. After a life-altering spiritual awakening, she returned to California, earned a Master's degree in Marriage, Family, and Child Therapy, and became a Certified Expressive Arts Therapist.

Anita went on to co-found the Art Center at the Esalen Institute in Big Sur, California, where she led groups in energy healing and Expressive Therapy. Later, she founded the Glen House Healing Center in Sausalito and created the *Energy Awareness Training Series*. She became known for her original therapeutic approach, "*Telenergy*"—a unique integration of psychotherapy, energy healing, and channeled counseling.

The author of an inspirational children's book titled *The Rainbow of Hope*, Anita now lives in San Miguel de Allende, Mexico, where she continues to write, dance, and offer spiritual intuitive counseling. She has served as a healer and counselor for nearly forty years.